The
Color of Desire

—

Hurricane

BOOKS BY NILO CRUZ AVAILABLE FROM TCG

Anna in the Tropics

Ana en el Trópico

Beauty of the Father

The Color of Desire / Hurricane

Two Sisters and a Piano and Other Plays
INCLUDES:
A Bicycle Country
Capricho
Hortensia and the Museum of Dreams
Lorca in a Green Dress

The
Color of Desire

—

Hurricane

TWO PLAYS

Nilo Cruz

THEATRE COMMUNICATIONS GROUP
NEW YORK
2011

The Color of Desire and *Hurricane* are published by
Theatre Communications Group, Inc.,
520 Eighth Avenue, 24th Floor, New York, NY 10018-4156

The publication of *The Color of Desire / Hurricane* through TCG's Book Program is made possible in part by the New York State Council on the Arts with the support of Governor Andrew Cuomo and the New York State Legislature.

TCG books are exclusively distributed to the book trade by Consortium Book Sales and Distribution.

LIBRARY OF CONGRESS CATALOGING-IN-PUBLICATION DATA
Cruz, Nilo.
The color of desire [and] Hurricane / Nilo Cruz—1st ed.
p. cm.
ISBN 978-1-55936-402-7
I. Title.
PS3603.R895C65   2011
812'.6—dc23   2011034935

Book, cover design and composition by Lisa Govan
Cover painting by Sandro de la Rosa
First Edition, December 2011

Love is so short,
forgetting is so long.

—Pablo Neruda,
"Tonight I Can Write"

Contents

The
Color of Desire

PRODUCTION HISTORY

The Color of Desire was produced at the Actors' Playhouse at the Miracle Theatre (Barbara S. Stein, Executive Director; David Arisco, Artistic Director) in Coral Gables, Florida, on October 8, 2010. It was directed by David Arisco; the scenic design was by Sean McClelland, the costume design was by Ellis Tillman, the lighting design was by Patrick Tennent and the sound design was by Alexander Herrin; the production stage manager was Carl Waisanen. The cast was as follows:

ALBERTINA	Teresa Maria Rojas
LEANDRA	Isabel Moreno
BELÉN	Hannia Guillen
PRESTON	Jim Ballard
ORLANDO	Sandor Juan
CAROLINE	Barbara Sloan
OSCAR	Michael Serratore
WAITER, EMCEE, YOUNG MAN	Nick Duckart

Characters

ALBERTINA: A Cuban woman, fifty-six

LEANDRA: A Cuban woman, her sister, sixty-eight

BELÉN: A Cuban woman, Albertina and Leandra's niece, mid-twenties

PRESTON: An American man, forties

ORLANDO: A Cuban man, late thirties/early forties

CAROLINE: An American woman, fifties

OSCAR: An Italian-American man, Caroline's lover, fifties

WAITER, EMCEE, YOUNG MAN: A Cuban man, twenty-eight

Setting

A solid back wall with louver doors that can be used for several locations: a costume shop, a nightclub and the living room of a house. Sound, light and objects should define the different locations. The sequences in italics indicate when the characters reenact and reinvent the past.

Author's Notes

The world you are about to enter is Havana, Cuba. The time is 1960, a year after the revolution. This was a moment of transition for the island, which was still in a state of war, fighting terrorism from within its population and struggling with a vestigial past and an unsettling future.

The air in Havana was thick with the rising tension of suspicion and foreboding. The new government had to come up with makeshift solutions to facilitate the changeover, promulgating a campaign involving ordinary workers in bars and servants in private houses to denounce any individuals who were against the new system. The Committees for the Defense of the Revolution was also created to monitor the activities of each person in his respective block and to report any "counterrevolutionary" activity.

By late 1960, the National Institute for Agrarian Reform controlled more than half the industrial structure of the island, and virtually halted all private building by establishing the Urban Reform Law. In addition, the government ran the theatres, cinemas, television centers and musical activities.

Act One

SCENE I

The Aunts

Lights reveal Leandra and Albertina at a costume shop in a theatre. They are folding old theatre curtains.

LEANDRA: It's getting dark outside. There's such a sad presence about October.

ALBERTINA: It's probably because the light gets dimmer this time of the year.

LEANDRA: I always think October should be taken out of the calendar. And November, too. But not December, because in December we have Christmas and people get festive and happy, and we also get a little breeze.

ALBERTINA: If you take October out of the calendar I wouldn't have a birthday.

LEANDRA: That's not necessarily a bad thing, keeps you from aging.

ALBERTINA: I want to get old like everyone else.

LEANDRA: Well, old, you already are.

(Albertina gives her a look.)

ALBERTINA: But I want to have the pleasure of getting older than you, and to have the satisfaction of stretching my legs when my time comes.

LEANDRA *(Refers to curtains)*: I don't know why they're having us mend all these rags.

ALBERTINA: Yes, they've seen better days.

LEANDRA: They do it to save money.

ALBERTINA: They do it because they have no money.

LEANDRA *(Sighs and looks up)*: Ah, what I wouldn't give to be acting again!

ALBERTINA: That makes two of us.

LEANDRA: You stand more chances than I do. With this bad leg, beggars and pirates are all I'll be able to play.

ALBERTINA: Two seasons without work. The least the company could've done was to give us the part of the understudies . . . if they had understudies.

LEANDRA: God forbid! Knowing me I'd start wishing the actors the flu so I get to go on.

ALBERTINA: Ay, Leandra, that's evil.

LEANDRA: Remember that at my age I only have a few nights left in the theatre.

(Belén, their niece, wearing a mustache, enters, holding a box.)

BELÉN: I found the box with the mustaches. It was on the last shelf behind the box with the wigs. You think José Antonio would like this mustache for the king?

ALBERTINA: No, too 1800s.

BELÉN: And this one?

ALBERTINA: Too Sherlock Holmes.

LEANDRA: The king should have a beard, gray and long, down to his chest.

BELÉN: What do you think of this mustache for Rosaura?

(Belén tries on another mustache and begins to enact one of Rosaura's monologues from Life Is a Dream.*)*

Noble Prince, three times I have appeared before you in different guise and form. Three times . . .

LEANDRA AND BELÉN:

. . . The first you mistook me for a man, you were a prisoner in chains, and my pain seemed like nothing compared to your misery.

LEANDRA: I remember that monologue when I did it! How young was I then!

BELÉN: How young?

LEANDRA: Your age.

BELÉN *(Disappointedly)*: So I will never play Rosaura.

LEANDRA: Oh, my child, there'll be other opportunities.

ALBERTINA: Well, if it's any consolation . . . I always had doubts about men who fall in love with girls disguised as boys.

LEANDRA: Me, too. And what's more confusing is when a man plays a woman who disguises herself as a man.

ALBERTINA: Yes, that must be a real anatomical puzzle for the audience! Haven't you noticed that when women get older we start looking more like men?

LEANDRA: That's because old age is ruthless and doesn't give a damn what sex we are.

ALBERTINA: And have I started looking like a man?

LEANDRA *(Playfully)*: Uh-hum, and the only thing you need is a beard. Come on, let's talk about other things; you know how susceptible I am about old age. And today of all days I ran out of cold cream.

BELÉN *(Looks up)*: Listen to them. They started rehearsals upstairs. Everything hurts when I hear Heloisa stumble through her lines. I know I should wish her well. But when

I think I was never given a chance to play that role, my blood boils with indignation!

(Belén exits with the box of mustaches.)

ALBERTINA: She's not taking this well.
LEANDRA: That damn José Antonio! He should've given her the role.
ALBERTINA: I told her this had nothing to do with her talent, that it was all politics.

(Belén reenters holding a dress.)

BELÉN: I'm going to borrow this from the shop.
LEANDRA: That's an expensive dress.
BELÉN: I'll wear it this evening and return it tomorrow.

(Belén tries on the dress.)

LEANDRA: I don't want to get in trouble with José Antonio.
BELÉN: You won't. He'll be busy with his rehearsal.
LEANDRA: Where are you going?
BELÉN: To distract myself a little.
LEANDRA: Alone?
BELÉN: No. An American man has expressed interest in me.
LEANDRA: And who is this gentleman?
BELÉN: Tía Berta met him the other day. She can tell you all about him.

(Belén goes out.)

LEANDRA: Who's this man?
ALBERTINA: It's the American man I told you about. I even told you his name so you'd remind me.
LEANDRA: And who do you think I am, your secretary?

ALBERTINA: I think he's a director or a producer. I asked him if he had a role for me, and when he said no I didn't bother to ask him anything else.

LEANDRA: You're just as bad as I am.

ALBERTINA: What can I say! I'm an actress, and if there's no part for me, I don't ask!

(Belén reenters wearing a shawl.)

BELÉN: I'm leaving.

ALBERTINA: You look lovely.

LEANDRA: Is he coming to pick you up so I can meet him?

BELÉN: No. I'm meeting him at Monsignor.

LEANDRA: You ought to introduce him to me. After all you live under my roof.

ALBERTINA: Let her be, Nanda. Go out the back door. Make sure José Antonio doesn't see you wearing the dress.

BELÉN: Don't worry if he sees me, I'll tell him that I'm just an illusion.

LEANDRA: Come here, Belén. Is this man someone we can trust? Is he respectable?

BELÉN: Adiós, Tía Nanda.

(Belén exits.)

LEANDRA: It would be good if he has good intentions.

ALBERTINA: Nanda, don't get ahead of yourself.

LEANDRA: An American man would be good for her. God knows what's going to happen in this country, and I pray we could get her out of this place.

ALBERTINA: From your mouth to God's ear.

(Lights change.)

Scene 2

The American Man

At a nightclub. Preston is dressed in an elegant suit. Dance music plays in the background. A Waiter enters.

WAITER: One of your guests is here to see you.
PRESTON: Send her this way.

(The Waiter escorts Belén in, then exits.)

BELÉN: I thought you'd be at the other bar.
PRESTON: No, too many people on the other side. I'm glad you
     decided to come.
BELÉN: Me, too. *(She walks to conceal her nervousness)* I like the
     music.
PRESTON: Were you busy rehearsing today?
BELÉN: No, I didn't manage to get the role I wanted.
PRESTON: That's a shame. You seemed so right for it.

BELÉN: Nothing to be done. I've forgotten all about it. This afternoon at three o'clock, to be exact, I erased it from my mind. *(Smiles)* Zooom . . . gone from life. It's not an easy world the theatre!

PRESTON: Then why are you in it?

BELÉN: I can't think of doing anything else.

PRESTON: Is that because you like being more than one person?

BELÉN: Yes, you can say that.

PRESTON: And you like embodying that many lives? And you like living that much?

BELÉN: Probably as much as you do . . . *(Smiles)* Unless, you're suicidal.

PRESTON *(Laughs)*: No, I'm not suicidal

BELÉN *(Laughing with him)*: I didn't think you were. A dark cloud surrounds people who are in despair.

PRESTON *(Playfully)*: Well, it's hard to see dark clouds in the night.

(They both laugh.)

BELÉN: Tell me a little about yourself.

PRESTON: You mean about growing up in Portland? Or about coming here with my family when I was a boy?

BELÉN: About your childhood here.

PRESTON: Well, my grandfather used to say that Portland was a good place to bring up a family, and Cuba was the place to grow old and die. So I decided to follow his advice.

BELÉN: But you're not going to die any time soon.

PRESTON: I hope not. *(Smiles)* I've been coming here since I was a child. My grandfather had a rum distillery. I was baptized here with sugarcane juice.

BELÉN: What a sweet way to be baptized.

PRESTON: I think rum would've been better!

(They both laugh. The Waiter enters with Preston's friends, Caroline and Oscar.)

WAITER: Right this way. *(After a nod to Preston, he exits)*

CAROLINE: Preston, we found you!

OSCAR: How are you, my friend!

CAROLINE: How do you do! I'm Caroline.

PRESTON: Caroline and Oscar, this is Belén.

OSCAR: Glad to meet you.

BELÉN: My pleasure.

CAROLINE: Isn't it splendid tonight! I can never get enough of this place. When we left New York, it was starting to get chilly. Can you believe it, so early in the fall?! And it was nippy as far as Georgia. Don't tell anybody, but I was shivering on the ship's deck in my old coat.

OSCAR: She wanted to buy a new coat before we left New York.

CAROLINE: And I should've bought it!

OSCAR: You've got more than six hanging in your closet. What do you need so many coats for?

CAROLINE: And they're all falling apart. They look like old pieces of pelt, hair falling all over the place, shedding everywhere.

OSCAR: Do you think Caroline would ever keep a coat that's falling apart?

CAROLINE: I simply look like a cavewoman every time I wear them.

OSCAR: Can you believe her! Do you think she'll ever look like a cavewoman?

CAROLINE *(To Belén)*: Isn't he a bore! I should've just pushed him off the deck so the sharks could've enjoyed a good meal. Men don't understand that when we buy a dress what we're actually buying is the occasion to wear it. We're buying a night like this one.

OSCAR: The problem with you, my dear, is that you always wind up buying the whole store.

CAROLINE: And you love it when I look divine.

OSCAR: Yes, I love it when you look divine.

CAROLINE *(Hits him with her gloves)*: You devil! *(To Belén)* Accompany me to the powder room, dear!

(Belén and Caroline exit.)

PRESTON: What brings you to the island so early this year?

OSCAR: It's the only time we're able to get away.

PRESTON: Things here are getting worse by the day.

OSCAR: That's what I was afraid of.

PRESTON: It's definitely not getting any better for Americans like us. For the last five months I've been living out of a suitcase, ready to leave if things don't get any better.

OSCAR: That bad?

PRESTON: The government is nationalizing practically all the businesses, and I happen to have a business, my friend. Not particularly lucrative at this moment. As you can see, there are only a few migratory snowbirds in this place, because not many people are traveling here and I'm in the migratory business.

OSCAR: The casinos should've never been closed.

PRESTON: Oh, they just wanted to get rid of the mobsters who were running the show. Now they've reopened them, and they're doing business with the same old thugs they wanted to get rid of in the first place. You know if I were Caroline I'd get rid of the house here.

OSCAR: Oh, she wouldn't do that. It was her father's house, and it's been in the family for years.

(The Waiter enters with a few appetizers.)

WAITER: Here's something to nibble on, courtesy of the house.

PRESTON: Gracias.

(A bolero begins to play. Caroline and Belén enter, involved in conversation.)

BELÉN: Some people think shells hold secrets, and they use them to foretell the future.

CAROLINE: Do you know how to read the future yourself?

BELÉN: No. But I wish I did.

CAROLINE: I don't. I want to live moment to moment. If I knew what's coming my way, then I would feel the future is kidnapping my present.

BELÉN: Sometimes I'd like to know where I'm heading.

CAROLINE: Are you referring to your relationship with Preston?

BELÉN: Oh no, I haven't known him for that long.

CAROLINE: Well, it's hard to get to know men. They're not very open.

BELÉN: Do you know if he's married?

CAROLINE: Of course, darling. Except Preston was destined for the life of a divorcé, that's why he likes to live here where there's more freedom. Then again, I don't think his wife would ever grant him a divorce. But none of this matters, dear. Look at Oscar and me . . . we're not married. You just have faith in your intuition and tread carefully.

WAITER: Anything else, señores?

OSCAR: Two martinis.

WAITER: And for you, señor?

PRESTON: No, thank you.

(The Waiter exits.)

CAROLINE: The band started playing. I'm ready to dance. Let's go, Oscar.

OSCAR: But we just got in.

CAROLINE: I want to dance.

OSCAR: Do you always have to be so bossy?

CAROLINE: I'm just looking forward to having a good time. Come on, lovey-dovey!

(They go off to dance. Preston goes to Belén.)

PRESTON: Are you enjoying yourself?

BELÉN: Well, this is all very new to me.

PRESTON: But are you having fun?

BELÉN: Yes, I can say that I am.

PRESTON: That's what matters. *(He touches her face)* You're lovely. You know that?

BELÉN: No.

PRESTON: Well you are.

(He lifts her chin and kisses her on the mouth.)

Shall we dance?

(He offers his hand. She takes it. They walk off to the dance floor. Lights change.)

SCENE 3

Preparations

Lights reveal Albertina and Leandra at the costume shop.

ALBERTINA *(Reading from a list)*: Estrella's dress needs to be
    shortened.
LEANDRA: Check.
ALBERTINA: New beard for Basilio.
LEANDRA: Check.
ALBERTINA: Find new beard for Segismundo.
LEANDRA: How many beards does he think we have?
ALBERTINA: I don't know.
LEANDRA: So what does he expect?
ALBERTINA: I have no idea.
LEANDRA: He didn't tell you what shape of beard he wants?
ALBERTINA: No.
LEANDRA: What's wrong with you today?!
ALBERTINA: I have colic.

LEANDRA: Colic is what babies have.

ALBERTINA: Then a baby with colic I must have. *(Drinks from a glass)*

LEANDRA: That's all we need, you pregnant at your age. What's that stuff you're drinking?

ALBERTINA: Seltzer.

LEANDRA: When you're finished tell José Antonio to get the beard he wants, himself. All he has to do is walk down the street and pluck out the beard of the first militiaman he finds.

ALBERTINA: All right. Check. I'll let him know you said that. Anything else?

(Belén enters.)

BELÉN: Good morning!

ALBERTINA: How was it last night?

BELÉN: Good. He's an interesting man.

ALBERTINA: And with enough money to buy us a theatre . . . I know all about it. He owns a shipping company, and his grandfather had a rum distillery in Colón. So what happened?

BELÉN *(Playfully, as if hiding a secret)*: Nothing you'll need to know.

LEANDRA: Hum. Sounds promising.

BELÉN: I had the best time last night! From now on I shall start a new life with him. I shall wear expensive perfume and dine in fine restaurants. *(Laughs, swivels full of joy)* And I shall be seen at the Havana Yacht Club sipping daiquiris with his friends from New York.

LEANDRA: Really? And when will I meet this American man?

BELÉN: One of these days.

LEANDRA: Where did he take you last night?

BELÉN: To the Montmartre and the Copa Room.

ALBERTINA: Aren't you glad we're not like those pesky chaperones that sit in dance halls spying, looking like prehistoric iguanas that have infrared eyesight and German shepherd hearing?

LEANDRA: It would be good if he has good intentions and he finds a place for you in his heart. I pray to God we could get you out of this country.

BELÉN: Is that all you want, Tía Nanda, to marry me off?

LEANDRA: No, my child. But everyone says there's going to be an American invasion, and there's talk of the government sending young people to Russia and Czechoslovakia. I'm afraid if you stay here you might end up in one of those countries. Helena from across the street has found a way of sending her children to the states.

ALBERTINA: Sssshhhh . . . Not so loud, Nanda.

LEANDRA: There's no one here. Everybody is upstairs rehearsing.

ALBERTINA: Then go ahead and shout so everyone can hear you!

LEANDRA (Dismissively): It's bad enough I wasted a year of my life in silence. Do you know what it's like not to talk for a year?

ALBERTINA: Yes. And I preferred when you were silent.

LEANDRA: Well, I don't wish what I had on anybody! Praise the Lord, when the words came back! When they started to appear on the doorway of my mouth once again. Yes, sometimes I'd say the wrong things. I'd tell people I had aphasia, and they'd understand I had a facial. I'd ask the doctor, "What are your plans for me?" And he'd understand, "Water the plants for me." But now . . . now the words have become obedient; so I can talk all I want, and say things as they are, even if they take me to jail.

ALBERTINA: Yes, it's because of that tongue of yours we're stuck in this costume shop. If you hadn't said the things you said against the revolutionaries, we'd still be acting on the stage.

LEANDRA: If you could get this man to do something for you then you're saved, my child!

BELÉN: But what about the two of you?

ALBERTINA: I don't know about her, but I already have a master plan for myself.

LEANDRA: What's important is your safety. We've already lived our lives.

ALBERTINA: Speak for yourself!

BELÉN: I wouldn't want to leave without you.

LEANDRA: Don't worry about us. One day you'll have to go from our side and it might as well happen now before it's too late. We'll put everything inside a suitcase and you'll get on with your life. You'll close the door behind you and we'll manage.

(The aunts start to exit.)

ALBERTINA: Rehearsal is starting. We better go upstairs and take all the props to the cast.

(Belén stays, lost in thought, then leaves.
Lights change.)

SCENE 4

The Interpreter

At the nightclub. Dance music plays. Orlando and Preston are having a heated discussion.

PRESTON: But you can't tell a man to get out of the way!

ORLANDO: Why not?

PRESTON: Because that's like punishing the rich so the poor can get ahead in life.

ORLANDO: So you want the rich to stay rich and the rest of humanity is doomed.

PRESTON: I just think we have to find a happy medium in this country.

ORLANDO: You have to be more of a visionary.

PRESTON: Let's not confuse visionaries with extremists!

ORLANDO *(Laughs)*: Extremists? Us?

PRESTON *(Grins)*: I don't like what happened to Michael Goodwin.

ORLANDO: He's counterrevolutionary

PRESTON: He's no such thing.

ORLANDO: How would you know?

PRESTON: He's a friend of mine.

ORLANDO: A terrorist would never reveal his true identity.

PRESTON: And you think that's right what they did to him?

ORLANDO: They were following orders.

PRESTON: What orders? He's in critical condition and he's not even responding. They're a bunch of bullies. A bunch of youngsters who have joined the military. I'm getting tired of living in an atmosphere of suspicion, Orlando. We both know that if this information gets to the media, it could affect the whole tourist industry. And if this kind of violence continues, the tourists won't come back here, especially American tourists.

ORLANDO: So let us repair some of the damage that's been done.

(Beat. Orlando pats him on the shoulder.)

PRESTON: Really? How are you going to do that?

ORLANDO: We want to restructure the tourist commission, and I think you'd be the perfect candidate for the job.

PRESTON: Really? So you want to put my American face in the tourist commission so everything looks fine and dandy.

ORLANDO: Nonsense.

PRESTON: I'm not stupid, Orlando.

ORLANDO: We're interested in you, Preston! And you're the man for this job.

PRESTON: Look, God knows I'd like to stay here and make things happen.

ORLANDO: Then let me talk to the guys and arrange a meeting with the whole collective.

PRESTON: And this commission . . . is Jimenez in charge of putting it together?

ORLANDO: We're all trying to recruit people.

PRESTON: And do these guys know who I am and where I come from?

ORLANDO: I wouldn't be here if they didn't.

PRESTON: So what kind of position are you offering me?

ORLANDO: We would have to negotiate.

PRESTON: I have my terms, Orlando.

ORLANDO: So do we.

PRESTON *(With a grin)*: I hope you don't intend for me to become a civil servant and wear fatigues.

ORLANDO *(With irony)*: No, we know you like to wear your linen suits. But you might have to change your style a little and accommodate to our new system. I'll tell the guys you're interested in the job and they should talk to you. *(Pats him on the shoulder again)*

(The Waiter enters.)

WAITER *(To Preston)*: Your guest is here, señor.

ORLANDO: Come by the office on Thursday.

(Belén enters.)

Enjoy yourselves.

(Orlando leaves.)

BELÉN: I'm late. I had to stay after rehearsals.

(He kisses her on the cheek.)

PRESTON: They sure keep you busy at that theatre.

BELÉN: Yes, but not the way I'd like to. Believe me, I'd much rather be on a stage than sewing in a costume shop.

(He brings her closer to him.)

PRESTON: You really miss acting, don't you?

BELÉN: Yes.

PRESTON: How much?

BELÉN: Like a lost lover.

PRESTON: Maybe we can do something about it.

BELÉN: Do you own a theatre?

PRESTON (*With a grin*): No. But how about playing for a one-member audience?

BELÉN: And who would that audience member be, the Queen of England?

PRESTON: No. Me.

BELÉN: And who do you want me to play?

PRESTON: A fantasy.

BELÉN: Are you confusing me with a call girl?

PRESTON: That's not my intention. I didn't mean to offend you.

(She moves away from him. He takes her by the arm.)

BELÉN: I gather you want me to play a woman.

PRESTON: It would be a waste if I'd ask you to play a man.

BELÉN: It's not every day I'm asked to do something like this. Do I know her?

PRESTON: Yes.

BELÉN: Who is she?

PRESTON: Someone . . . someone who was part of my past. You remind me of her.

BELÉN: Who is this woman?

PRESTON: Her name is Emilia.

BELÉN: Emilia Naguid, the actress?

PRESTON: Yes.

BELÉN: We are very different she and I.

PRESTON: I don't know you well enough to tell the difference.

BELÉN: Then get to know me.

(She moves away from him.)

PRESTON: Look, it's better this way. I mean . . . for now.

BELÉN: So I shouldn't try to love you.

PRESTON: I'd much rather if you didn't.

BELÉN: And what good would this do you?

PRESTON: It's not important. I just know I couldn't help asking you.

BELÉN: I can never be her.

PRESTON: What can I do to convince you?

BELÉN: Nothing.

(She walks away from him.)

PRESTON: Afraid?

BELÉN: I've never done anything like this before.

PRESTON: You know what some actors say about fear?

BELÉN: You're not offering me a role in the theatre.

PRESTON: I'll guide you.

BELÉN: And what would I get in return for doing this?

PRESTON: Anything you like.

BELÉN: Anything?

PRESTON: Absolutely.

BELÉN *(Grins)*: I might ask for the moon.

PRESTON: Then the moon it is.

BELÉN: My aunts think I should leave the country. Can you help me? Can you help me get out?

PRESTON: I can certainly try.

(She turns to him. She studies him: his good looks, his suit, his wristwatch. Her curiosity surfaces.)

BELÉN: Then I'll play Emilia.

PRESTON: All right then. Let's toast to fantasy.

*(They start to exit as a bolero begins to rise.
Lights change.)*

Scene 5

Searching for Emilia Naguid

At the costume shop. Leandra and Albertina enter pushing a costume rack.

LEANDRA: Here's a list of things they need for today.

ALBERTINA: Ah, so now the king has a beard! Good. I'm keeping his mustache then.

LEANDRA: What do you want a mustache for?

ALBERTINA: In case.

LEANDRA: In case what?

ALBERTINA: In case I need it.

LEANDRA: And what are you going to do with a mustache?

ALBERTINA: Lydia might get me a fake passport to leave the country. It might be a man's passport.

LEANDRA: So you're going to disguise yourself as a man?

ALBERTINA: Sure, if I have to. I'm not staying here.

LEANDRA: And you think it's as easy as putting on a mustache in a play?

ALBERTINA: Why not? Look, I'm already practicing my walk.

(She demonstrates her walk.)

LEANDRA: Oh Lord! I can see how you're gonna make your grand exit: straight to prison for leaving the country illegally.

(Belén enters holding a dress.)

BELÉN: José Antonio doesn't like the dress.

LEANDRA: What's wrong with it?

BELÉN: He thinks it's ugly and wrong for the play.

LEANDRA: I made exactly what he asked me to make. Ugh! One day I shall go upstairs and tell that manic good-for-nothing director I'm through!

ALBERTINA: And you think he's gonna get down on his knees and beg you not to quit? We missed our chance to make our grand exit. We are old and the theatre can manage without us.

LEANDRA: I'm going upstairs to talk to him.

(Leandra exits.)

ALBERTINA: What time did you get home last night?

BELÉN: Late.

ALBERTINA: How did it go?

BELÉN: It's hard to explain. I know you won't understand. I don't even understand it myself.

ALBERTINA: Why is that?

(Belén looks at Albertina and hesitates.)

BELÉN: Well I . . . I kind of remind him of someone else, someone who was part of his past, so the attraction isn't mutual.

ALBERTINA: Did he tell you this?

BELÉN: I could see the face projected on his eyes and it wasn't my face.

ALBERTINA: That's no good.

BELÉN: But I want him, Tía Berta.

ALBERTINA: So you've accepted all this?

BELÉN: Maybe I could make him see me for who I am.

ALBERTINA: You do realize he wants you to be someone else— someone who you're not.

BELÉN: I'll make him love me.

ALBERTINA: Not when he's got some other woman stuck in his mind! Some memories never really go away. They just take on other forms, like insects caught in amber!

BELÉN: Just think of it this way . . . this could be one way of getting out of this place.

ALBERTINA: But you can't be part of a bargain!

BELÉN: You want to marry me well, don't you?

ALBERTINA: Yes, but I don't want you to prostitute yourself.

BELÉN *(With determination)*: I want him and I'll make him love me.

(Albertina is horrified.)

ALBERTINA: In that case you won't hear any advice.

BELÉN: Please. Just tell me what you know about Emilia Naguid.

ALBERTINA: Your Aunt Nanda knew her better than I did.

BELÉN: But you were close to her at the beginning when she joined the company.

ALBERTINA: That's true. But I don't know if she would've chosen me as a friend.

BELÉN: Did she ever tell you about her lover Hugo?

ALBERTINA: Oh, why are you getting me into this? *(Lowers her head in shame)* It's so awful that everything's come to this!

BELÉN: Please, it's my only chance. Tell me what you know about Emilia.

ALBERTINA: I only know that she was miserable because Batista's men killed her lover. Well, it was never clear he was dead. That's what made it so painful for her.

BELÉN: So you think that's why she left the country?

(Leandra enters but stays at a distance, listening.)

ALBERTINA: Well, some people say that sometimes she wanted her pain to equal the violence all around us. The same violence we have now with the firing squads.

BELÉN: Don't tell Tía Nanda that we've had this conversation.

(Leandra enters. She fixes her eyes on Belén, then looks at Albertina.)

LEANDRA *(To Belén)*: Get me the blue material I bought. I have to make a new dress for that bastard.

(Belén exits.)

What were you two so secretive about?

ALBERTINA: Nothing important.

LEANDRA: You're lying.

ALBERTINA: It's nothing you'll want to know.

LEANDRA: Don't be hiding things from me!

ALBERTINA: Nothing can be kept from you, Nanda.

LEANDRA: Then come out with it!

ALBERTINA: You want her to marry well and get out of this place?!

LEANDRA: Of course I do.

ALBERTINA: Then you ought to know she's doing all she can do.

LEANDRA: That's not enough information.

ALBERTINA: That's all I can tell you. I'm going to the rehearsal.

(Albertina exits.
Lights change.)

Scene 6

Losing the Tropical Light

Afternoon. Oscar and Caroline are at the nightclub, drinking. Dance music plays. Caroline wears a large hat and a long scarf.

CAROLINE: So what's the point going on about it?

OSCAR: I just can't stop thinking about the letter.

CAROLINE: I tore it up and put in the trash.

OSCAR: You didn't.

CAROLINE: Of course. The new government can't take away my house. It's my property.

OSCAR: Caroline, this place has changed, and we don't know the new laws.

CAROLINE: Is that all you care about, my losing my house?

OSCAR: If they take away your house, we won't have a place to be with each other.

CAROLINE: Oscar, today I'd like to forget everything that's happening here. Why don't we think of agreeable things that will lift our spirit? I don't know why, but I always feel a certain kind of liveliness when I come to Cuba. Today I was talking to Belén and I told her we're not married because we'd rather continue our relationship as a love affair. I even told her that you haven't asked me to marry because I have more money than you do, so you would rather prove your love to me. *(Slight pause)* Is that really the truth, Oscar?

OSCAR: Have I done something to make you think less of me?

CAROLINE: No. But I . . . I sometimes think you're only interested in the life I offer you.

OSCAR: Now you're being offensive.

CAROLINE: I'm sorry . . . I . . . I didn't it mean it that way.

OSCAR: Of course you did! You're just as offensive as your mother who won't give you a penny if you marry someone like me.

CAROLINE: I'm sorry. Please . . .

OSCAR: I work hard for my own money for you to tell me something like that. Do I still have to prove myself to you?

CAROLINE: Yes. I mean no . . . No.

OSCAR: Madonna! Proprio matta de legare!

CAROLINE: Are you upset? I know when you get upset. You start speaking Italian like your father.

OSCAR: Ma basta! Quanto rompi!

CAROLINE: I know you just said something awful to me. Translate it!

OSCAR: I'm too upset to translate anything!

CAROLINE: It always sounds worse when you curse to me in Italian.

OSCAR: Good! Fai sempre cosí. Non è la prima volta. And you do it to bother me. Ah, the hell with everything! Basta! Finito! End of story!

(Caroline signals the Waiter.)

CAROLINE: Waiter!

(The Waiter enters.)

WAITER: Si, señora.

CAROLINE: Get me a martini. No. Make it two martinis.

WAITER: Two martinis coming up for the señora.

OSCAR *(To the Waiter)*: Don't give her any martinis. *(He gives him money)* Give them to me.

WAITER: Yes, sir.

CAROLINE *(Trying to get back at Oscar)*: I'd like to order two mojitos, if the gentleman is drinking martinis.

OSCAR: Just bring her a pitcher of water.

WAITER *(Rolls his eyes, mumbles as he leaves)*: ¡Estos americanos locos!

(Oscar takes a sip of his drink. Silence.)

CAROLINE *(As if nothing has happened)*: Maybe a dream rendezvous is the best thing for us.

OSCAR: What is that, another cruise ship?

CAROLINE: No, it's people meeting up in dreams, having a rendezvous.

OSCAR: It's more likely we'll have a nightmare.

CAROLINE: Oh, Oscar, if anybody heard you, they'd think we're always at war.

OSCAR: We are.

CAROLINE: Forget it! Where's the waiter?

OSCAR: No. What makes you think we'll get along better in a dream?

CAROLINE: First we will have to choose a dream. And we have to choose a meeting place in this dream, somewhere that seems pleasant to us. A place that is not over-intense or has negative associations for both of us . . .

OSCAR: That's nowhere.

CAROLINE: Oh, Oscar! I can think of many places.

OSCAR: Such as?

CAROLINE: Venice.

OSCAR: We had an awful fight there.
CAROLINE: Madrid.
OSCAR: I swore never to see you again.
CAROLINE: Oh, just forget it! You don't know how to dream.

(She starts to walk away.)

OSCAR: Hey, where are you going? What do I have to do to meet you in a dream?

(She leaves.)

(To himself) Cazzo!

(The Waiter enters with a tray full of drinks.)

WAITER: Your drinks, señor.
OSCAR: I don't want them. *(Dismissively)* Keep them! Make someone happy . . . or water the plants with them!

(Oscar exits. The Waiter is dumbfounded.)

WAITER *(To himself)*: ¡Americanos locos! ¡Locos de remate!

(Lights change.)

SCENE 7

The Object of Gravity

Preston's house. Belén enters, wearing an elegant gown and high-heeled shoes. She looks at herself in the mirror.

BELÉN: What else do I need to know about you? Would you wear this dress? These shoes? How do you walk? What is it I don't know about you? What other secrets do you possess?

(Preston enters. He walks over and looks at her through the mirror.)

PRESTON: You look lovely.

(She walks around the space, looking at everything.)

BELÉN: I like your place. You bring many girls to this place?

PRESTON *(Smiles)*: No.

BELÉN: So where did you meet with Emilia?

PRESTON: Different places.

BELÉN: And what are they like these places?

PRESTON: The government has closed them down.

BELÉN: And where do the lovers go now?

PRESTON *(With a smirk)*: I imagine they find other ways.

BELÉN: And the prostitutes?

PRESTON: I think that there's some kind of new program where they teach them things like reading and sewing.

BELÉN: Sewing!

(They both laugh.)

PRESTON: Tell me who you are now.

BELÉN: Emilia Naguid.

PRESTON: Come here.

(She moves closer. She becomes self-conscious.)

Let me look at you. *(She looks at him)* Don't be nervous.

BELÉN: This is all new to me. *(He kisses her shoulder)* I don't know her the way you did.

PRESTON: Emilia was different.

BELÉN: How did she love you?

PRESTON: She was looking to find someone she had lost in me.

BELÉN: You mean the student who had disappeared?

PRESTON: Yes, the same.

BELÉN: So you were her wound healer.

PRESTON: That's not important.

BELÉN: But it is.

PRESTON: You're an actress. Let yourself be taken. —Who are you now?

BELÉN: *Emilia Naguid.*

(He looks at her intently. She looks at him with the same intensity.)

PRESTON: *And where are you now?*

BELÉN: *In the room of darkness where you fill the abyss, and give it a form, a name . . . (Directly) Do you want to have me? I can't possibly give myself completely.*

PRESTON: *I knew this from the moment I met you. From the moment I noticed your eyes.*

I don't mind your sadness.

(He moves closer to her. He's about to kiss her.)

BELÉN: *No kissing.*

(He grabs her.)

PRESTON: *That's fine.*

BELÉN: *No hugging.*

PRESTON: *That's fine, too.*

BELÉN: *And don't tell me you love me.*

PRESTON: *I don't love you.*

BELÉN: *No sweet talk either.*

PRESTON *(He lets go of her)*: *We don't have to do this if you don't want to.*

BELÉN: *You're right. This is only a transaction.*

PRESTON: *You haven't asked for money.*

(She turns her back to him.)

BELÉN: *Undo me.*

(He unzips her dress. She stays in her slip. He takes money out of his wallet and gives it to her.)

PRESTON: *Is this enough?*

(Silence. She doesn't take his money.)

We can turn off the light if you want to. Or you can close your eyes.

(He starts to take off his shirt.)

BELÉN: *If I close my eyes, I'll see someone else.*
PRESTON: *Hugo? Is that who you want to see?*
BELÉN: *He's dead.*
PRESTON: *Have you been loved since this happened?*
BELÉN: *What kind of a question is that?*
PRESTON: *Have you been loved since you lost him?*

(She averts him.)

Was there someone else?
BELÉN: *Yes. There was someone . . .*
PRESTON: *Who?*
BELÉN: *A stranger.*
PRESTON: *Did he pay you?*
BELÉN: *Not with money.*
PRESTON: *Did he satisfy you?*
BELÉN: *I think so.*
PRESTON: *What did he do to please you? What does your pain taste like?*
BELÉN: *Hell.*
PRESTON: *What is hell?*
BELÉN: *Blood from a death squad.*
PRESTON: *What did this man do to please you?*

(Pause. She looks at him.)

BELÉN: *He let me see Hugo on his skin.*
PRESTON: *Is that what you want? You can imagine him by closing your eyes. Just close your eyes.*

(Gently he draws her to him. He glides down her body to her pelvis and embraces her.)

Where are you now?

BELÉN: *Where you allowed yourself to be taken every night.*
PRESTON: *What do you want?*
BELÉN: *You.*

(*She lowers herself to the floor. He lies on top of her, caressing her.*)

PRESTON: *Tell me you want me there between your legs.*
BELÉN: *I want you there where all my moisture gathers.*

(*They roll on the floor and he lets her sit on top of him. The lights fade. The lights come up again to illustrate the passage of time. Preston and Belén are lying on the floor, after making love.*)

I want to know if she ever loved you.
PRESTON: What does your instinct tell you?
BELÉN: Could you love me if Emilia wasn't there?
PRESTON: You would've met a different man.
BELÉN: I'd like to help you start loving again . . .

(*She moves closer to him. Outside we hear the sound of a car pulling into the driveway.*)

Somebody's outside.
PRESTON: No one's going to visit me at this hour.
BELÉN: I just heard a car.

(*There's a knock at the door.*)

I'll go get dressed.

(*She exits. Preston pulls on his pants, then opens the door. Orlando comes in.*)

ORLANDO: I need to talk to you.
PRESTON: You can't just come into my house in the middle of
the night!

ORLANDO: We have to talk. I had a conversation with Jimenez, and he told me he got into an argument with you.

PRESTON: We did have a little quarrel.

ORLANDO: He seemed pretty upset.

PRESTON: That's because we didn't agree on anything.

ORLANDO: I put myself on the line for you!

PRESTON: I didn't mean for you to get into trouble.

ORLANDO: But you agreed to talk to Jimenez and negotiate.

PRESTON: That's what I did, but we didn't get anywhere.

ORLANDO: Why don't you tell me your case against him?

PRESTON: I don't have a case against anybody. I just don't like how he wants to control me and use me as if I were a puppet.

ORLANDO: Nobody is trying to control you!

PRESTON: Of course he is!

ORLANDO: Listen to me. Get on our side, Preston! Join forces with us. I'm telling you, we can make something big happen in this country. Let me talk to him again.

PRESTON: And you think he's going to give a shit about what you tell him? He doesn't want me to run any tourist committee! He wants me to cross my arms and watch him run my fucking business into the ground.

ORLANDO: You want to learn the first rule about working with these guys . . . you keep your trap shut . . . and let them talk . . .

PRESTON: I don't need to know any of your damn rules. None of you guys know what the hell you're doing.

ORLANDO: Just listen to me . . .

PRESTON: Forget it! It's late.

ORLANDO: No, you listen to me! . . . This is not about doing your own shit and being on your own!

PRESTON: That's exactly what I don't like, Orlando. I don't like how this government wants to dominate everything: the banking system, the stores, the hotels, casinos, movie houses, the ports . . . the shitty tourist and shipping industry, which, you know very well, is my line of work!

ORLANDO: So what do you want from us? What do you want?

PRESTON: What any citizen would expect!

ORLANDO: And what is that according to you?

PRESTON: Respect! Respect for what is mine! Respect for the individual. You may have fallen for all these so-called revolutionary ideals. You might want to appear more proletariat than a carpenter, but I'm not going to fall for this crap!

ORLANDO: Let me just tell you something, you have two options here: you're either with us or not.

PRESTON: Then find someone else! Find someone else!

ORLANDO: All right, you're out then! You're out!

PRESTON: You're damn right I'm out! You're offering me nothing but crumbs . . . the crumbs of my own work.

ORLANDO: All right, compadre. I've made a mistake in you.

PRESTON: And I'm glad we got that straightened out.

(Orlando exits. Preston is distraught. Belén enters.)

BELÉN: What did he want?

PRESTON: You heard the conversation, didn't you?

BELÉN: A little bit.

(He paces the room. He's lost in thought, confused.)

PRESTON: They're making my life impossible. They want to see a man like me reduced to nothing.

BELÉN: There's nothing you can do.

PRESTON: I'm going to fight until the end. I'm not giving up.

(She goes to caress him.)

BELÉN: Come here.

(She tries to hug him from behind, but he doesn't let himself be touched.)

PRESTON: It's better if you go home.

BELÉN: Why?

PRESTON: I'm going out.

BELÉN: Where are you going at this hour?

PRESTON: I'm going to straighten this out.

BELÉN: Don't. Don't get into trouble with those guys.

PRESTON: I won't. Just go to your house.

(He starts putting on his shirt.)

BELÉN: Don't do it, Preston.

PRESTON: Just do what I'm telling you.

(He goes.)

BELÉN *(Calling out to him)*: Preston! Preston!

(We hear the sound of a car driving off. Belén stays motionless, looking in the direction in which Preston just left. Then she sits and lowers her head as the lights begin to shroud the room in darkness.
Lights change.)

Act Two

SCENE 1

The Mambo Contest

At the nightclub. Mambo music plays. The patrons start filing in. Caroline and Oscar enter and begin to dance. Leandra and Albertina enter, holding drinks and dancing, joyous. Preston and Belén enter. They start to dance. Then the music softens and the lights reveal an Emcee holding a microphone. Some move to tables, others remain standing to watch.

EMCEE: Señoras y señores, we will now have our third couple compete in tonight's contest. We have Caroline and Oscar. Are you enjoying your stay in our country? *(He extends the microphone)*

CAROLINE: Very much.

EMCEE: I imagine it's good to be away from the cold.

OSCAR: Nothing beats being in this part of the world this time of the year.

EMCEE: Oscar, you are from Italy, correct?

OSCAR: From the south, from Naples, but I live in America now . . . my feet in the United States and my heart always in Italy . . .

EMCEE: Caroline, were you born in the States?

CAROLINE: Yes, but I've been coming here since I was a child. I have a house here.

EMCEE: And are you married?

CAROLINE: No, in love . . .

EMCEE: Ah, in love! Good answer. Good for our Mambo Mango contest! Now you know the rules of the contest. We give you a mango. We'll place it under your chin, and you will have to make this mango seductive and inviting for Oscar here, because the mango and not the apple is the forbidden fruit.

CAROLINE: I'm ready!

EMCEE: Now Oscar, you will have to use your chin to obtain this delicious fruit that we'll place under Caroline's lovely chin, and you will try all this while dancing a mambo. *(He places the mango under her chin)* Is that clear?

OSCAR: We'll give it a try!

EMCEE: Are we ready?

(Caroline tries to nod but she can't.)

(To the audience) Are we ready?

(Caroline signals that she's ready.)

Let's hit it boys! Mambo #8.

(Mambo #8 begins to play. Oscar and Caroline begin to dance. Oscar tries to get the mango with his chin, but Caroline's breasts get in the way. She, in turn, tries to keep the fruit from falling off by lifting her chest. This makes it more difficult for Oscar to get to the mango. She tries to lean forward. He tries to go under her, but this makes his back hurt.)

Look at them, señoras y señores; they are like two lovebirds. Two doves in a mating dance. Look at what this forbidden fruit does to these lovers, the magnitude and force of the forbidden fruit, señoras y señores . . .

(All of a sudden the mango falls to the floor and the music comes to an end.)

Oh well, you didn't manage to get a bite of the forbidden fruit. But we're giving you the mango to take home as a souvenir. And for being such good sports, we're offering you two free drinks! And don't forget to try your luck at our casino. Maybe you were not lucky with our contest, but your fortune awaits you at the roulette table!

(Caroline and Oscar join Preston at his table.)

OSCAR: So we won a yellow mango.
PRESTON: You know what they say about mangoes, you have to eat them naked so you don't get the juice all over your clothes.

(They laugh.)

CAROLINE: Did you hear that, Oscar? We have to eat it naked.
OSCAR *(Jokingly)*: Here, in front of everybody? Okay! Give me the mango!

(He starts taking off his jacket and unbuckling his belt. The dialogue overlaps.)

ALBERTINA: No. Not here—!
LEANDRA: He didn't mean here—!
CAROLINE: I dare you—!
OSCAR: Give me the mango—!
ALBERTINA: No. Not here. Get down from the chair—!

OSCAR: Then where—?

LEANDRA: At home. At home with your wife—!

OSCAR: What wife—?

LEANDRA: Her.

CAROLINE: Oh, he's lost all the romance—!

OSCAR: She's the one who prefers a mango to me—

(She hits him with her gloves.)

CAROLINE: You fool!

OSCAR: All right! All right! Basta! Basta! These shows are terrible.

ALBERTINA: Oh, I had fun.

CAROLINE: We know that if we want to see showgirls with chandeliers on top of their heads we can go to Tropicana.

LEANDRA: I never get to go out, so for me this is a treat. Tonight I feel twenty years younger. I might walk out of this place without a cane.

BELÉN: Or with us holding you!

ALBERTINA: Leandra here, who seems to be modest tonight, but ate ten croquettes . . .

LEANDRA: I didn't eat ten croquettes!

BELÉN: You certainly did, Tía Nanda.

ALBERTINA: My sister here, is one of the greatest actresses in this town—

LEANDRA: In my good old days. But look at me now starting to look like a turtle, and with this damn cane, I can only play grandmothers and old servants in a Chekhov play. — But do tell me one thing, señores . . . did I really eat ten croquettes?

CAROLINE: No regrets! You enjoy yourself, darling . . .

LEANDRA: Well, in that case I'll have another drink and stay a while longer.

CAROLINE: Then let's go. Let's play a game of roulette at the casino, my treat, and you can't refuse my invitation. Let's go, maybe luck will come our way . . . Let's go. Let's go.

(The aunts start to exit with Caroline and Oscar.)

OSCAR: Aren't you coming?

BELÉN: You go ahead. I don't want to play tonight.

(Oscar exits.)

PRESTON: Your aunts are very charming.

BELÉN: It's strange being here with them.

PRESTON: Then why did you bring them?

BELÉN: They couldn't resist meeting the American man. *(He kisses her)* Why can't it always be like this?

PRESTON: How?

BELÉN: Without my having to live between the words of another woman. Why do you live on that loss?

PRESTON: If I hadn't met her you wouldn't have come to me.

(Orlando enters.)

ORLANDO: Buenas noches.

BELÉN: Buenas.

PRESTON: You didn't answer my telephone call.

ORLANDO: How dare you to go to Jimenez's house in the middle of the night!

PRESTON: I was as rude as you were when you showed up at my house. Did you bring that bastard with you?

ORLANDO: Hey, watch your mouth.

PRESTON: Did you bring that son of a bitch here with you?

ORLANDO: I'm telling you, control yourself. Lower your voice. I don't want any public scandals?

PRESTON: Scandal, me?

ORLANDO: You're overstepping your boundaries, Preston.

PRESTON: I noticed there's a table reserved for the commanders. Are you out celebrating?

ORLANDO: Just like you are.

PRESTON: I have nothing to celebrate. I'm just passing the time. So what brings you out this evening?

ORLANDO: Nothing you'll care to know. We just recruited another two hundred teachers to go to the countryside and teach people to read.

PRESTON: Congratulations. That's a lot of teachers.

ORLANDO: Not enough. We're labeling next year "The Year of Education."

PRESTON: Sounds impressive.

ORLANDO: It will be our most inspiring success. We're going to educate this whole country. *(To Belén)* Do you want to you join the theatre company we're putting together?

BELÉN: Me?

ORLANDO: Aren't you an actress? We could use your help. You'll be performing for the whole country.

BELÉN: You mean outdoor theatre?

ORLANDO: That's right. We need actors like you. We need all the help we can get.

PRESTON: I just heard that Jimenez is planning to take over another hundred and sixty-six companies.

ORLANDO: Yes, that's what he announced.

PRESTON: And mine is one of them, right?

ORLANDO: I don't have that information, Preston.

PRESTON: You certainly do!

ORLANDO: Preston, this is not the place!

PRESTON: You're lying! You work for the guy! How can you not know?

ORLANDO: It hasn't been publicly announced!

PRESTON: But it's official! *(Orlando shakes his head)* Why don't you just come out with it? Why don't you just tell me?

ORLANDO: Yes, your company is one of them.

PRESTON: I knew it! I saw it coming like a war.

ORLANDO: I couldn't do anything about it, but that's the reality.

(Preston grabs Orlando by his shirt collar. They struggle.)

PRESTON: Reality! You bastard!

ORLANDO: Hey, take it easy!

PRESTON: What gives you the right?!

(Orlando pushes him away.)

ORLANDO: Take it easy! It was a unanimous decision.

PRESTON: You're full of shit!

ORLANDO: I was looking out for you!

PRESTON: Looking out for me! You've had it in for me from the beginning!

ORLANDO: I wanted things to work out! We were all willing to work with you.

PRESTON: How? By making me into a puppet of your tourist committee? By keeping me as a floor sweeper in my own company! Is that how you were looking out for me? *(He takes out a handkerchief and dries the sweat from his forehead)*

ORLANDO: You gotta understand—

PRESTON: Understand what? What's their excuse this time? What's their excuse?

ORLANDO: They have no excuse.

PRESTON: I'm sure they don't.

ORLANDO: They said they won't allow you to continue running your company when other businesses have become government property.

PRESTON: That's bullshit!

ORLANDO: They said you represent the very idea of capitalism in this country, and if you want to stay on the island you would have to join the system.

PRESTON: And let them step all over me, after they stole from me?

ORLANDO: Look, you're still living a life of extravagance, which clashes with our system.

PRESTON: And what do you want me to become, a civil servant?

(Preston paces back and forth.)

ORLANDO: Listen, just know they're going to show up at your
office tomorrow.

PRESTON: Well, they're not welcomed! So spare them the visit!

ORLANDO: Look, I can understand how you'd be upset . . .

PRESTON: Upset?! I'm fucking furious!

BELÉN *(Intervening)*: Preston.

PRESTON: Go get your aunts. I'm going home. I'll give you a
ride to your house.

(Oscar enters. Belén stays.)

OSCAR: Caroline wants you to join them.

PRESTON: You remember Orlando.

OSCAR: Yes. How are you?

(They shake hands.)

PRESTON *(With irony)*: Orlando here just told me that the
National Institute for Reforms is going to take over my
business . . .

OSCAR: You're kidding!

PRESTON: Oh, it's official. It's official. They're going to nationalize it.

(Oscar looks at Orlando. Orlando looks at Preston.)

ORLANDO: That was private information, Preston.

PRESTON: What's so private about it! *(Pushes Orlando)* You're
fucking taking over my company! What's so private about
that! What's so private about it!

ORLANDO: I think I should go now. Buenas noches, señores.

(Orlando exits.)

PRESTON: Soon they'll nationalize everything, even the trees,
the air, the sand, the shade, the park benches. Even people's
words and thoughts!

OSCAR: Don't say that, Preston.

PRESTON: Oh, it's coming! It's coming! And faster than we think . . . It's happening as we speak. *(Paces)* It's revolting how everything can change from one day to the other, and what shocks me . . . what shocks me the most is the vulgar transformation!

OSCAR: But what I don't understand is that Americans are doing nothing about it, except putting a ban on all exports to the island.

PRESTON: And this is the response they're getting back, more American companies nationalized. I have to get the hell out of this country! I have to get out! *(Continues to pace back and forth as if lost)* I have to get out!

OSCAR *(Pats him on the shoulder)*: My friend, I'm sorry. I'm so sorry.

PRESTON: Oh, I knew it was coming! It's all over for us! Come here, Belén. *(He wraps his arm around her)*

(He is about to exit with Belén when Leandra enters.)

LEANDRA: They're losing. You should tell Caroline to stop splurging her money.

PRESTON: Ah, let her splurge. She can't take her money out of the country. It's all over for us.

OSCAR: Yes, he's right. Let her gamble. Let her gamble as much as she wants.

(Albertina and Caroline enter.)

ALBERTINA: We lost . . . we lost . . . Caroline wanted to continue playing but I don't want her to lose anymore money . . .

CAROLINE: Why not? It's of no use to us. We can't take our money out of the country!

OSCAR: That's right, and we might as well play. As we say in Italy: "Oggi in figura, domani in sepultura!" "Here today gone tomorrow! . . ."

CAROLINE: You know what I would like to do? I'd like to stand on the last floor of this hotel, like King Kong and start throwing my money to the people. Like this ... *(She throws a bunch of bills in the air)*

LEANDRA: No, you'll be arrested!—

CAROLINE: How can I be arrested for doing what I wish with my money!—

(They laugh.)

PRESTON: Because you're no longer allowed to do that in this country—

CAROLINE: Who says?! Look! Look!

(She throws more bills in the air.)

LEANDRA: Caroline, don't!

CAROLINE: Why would I be penalized? It's my money. Nobody here respects the laws that protect people's money.

ALBERTINA *(Laughing)*: Caroline! No. No ...

PRESTON: She's right! It's her damn money!

OSCAR *(Laughing)*: Sit down, Caroline. Don't be naughty, my love ...

(Oscar restrains Caroline.)

CAROLINE: Let go of me! Let go—!

PRESTON: Let her be. Let her do whatever she wants. It's her money.

(He throws some of his money into the air.)

Here's some more. It's worth nothing! Nothing! Nothing!

ALBERTINA *(Laughing)*: No, Preston. Don't throw away your money!

BELÉN: Preston, please ... don't!

*(Belén starts to pick up the money to give it back to Preston.
The others are picking up the bills as well. Oscar releases
Caroline, and the aunts hand her money back to Oscar.)*

CAROLINE: Ah, that felt so good. The release. I feel weightless.

LEANDRA: Somehow I fear the worst is yet to come, señores,
and there's going to be a war.

BELÉN: Ay, Tía Nanda, please, not now . . .

LEANDRA: No. No. I didn't say it. But I must confess I was
never a worrier. Except now, I've lost all peace of mind
and security. And those two things . . . those two things
have never abandoned me, not even in the theatre when
I've been left alone on a stage because an actor forgot
his entrance. —Well, now that you've heard my fatalism,
you'll probably think that I'm going straight to my house
and stick my head in the oven!

(She drinks the last of her cocktail.)

But no, tomorrow again, we'll have to face this bitter
comedy! And on that note, I take my leave! Enjoy the rest
of the evening!

PRESTON: Stay. We'll order more food and drinks.

LEANDRA *(Playfully)*: Ah, in that case.

ALBERTINA: No. No, we're going home.

LEANDRA: Good-bye, my friends.

CAROLINE: Good-bye, dear.

ALBERTINA: Good-bye. Thank you for such a nice evening.

LEANDRA: Do something for my niece, Mr. Preston, and take
her away from here. Islands are cursed. We are all cursed.

BELÉN: Let's go, Tía Nanda. Let's go. We'll walk you out.

(The Waiter enters with a tray of food.)

LEANDRA: Ah, is that more croquettes!

ALBERTINA: Let's go, Nanda.

(Preston, Belén and the two aunts exit.)

WAITER: Would you like anything else?

OSCAR: No, thank you. We'll take the check.

(The Waiter exits.)

CAROLINE: You want to go back to the casino?

OSCAR *(With playful sensuality)*: Or we can go home.

CAROLINE: And try to meet in a dream? You're not the best dreamer, my dear.

OSCAR: I do everything you tell me.

CAROLINE: You certainly can't remember me in your dreams.

OSCAR: So what's the big deal? I'd much rather see you in real life.

CAROLINE: Ohhh! Is that supposed to be a compliment, Oscar?

OSCAR: It's not a compliment. It's the truth! La verita. *(He kisses her)*

CAROLINE: Oh, Oscar, you rascal. Why did I meet you?

OSCAR: Because we are meant for each other, and I wish I could marry you.

CAROLINE: Let's just continue our relationship as a love affair, as if we're always at the beginning, and never reaching the end.

OSCAR: You see, I find you all over again here in Havana.

(Lights change.)

Scene 2

Pinning Saints

At the costume shop. Leandra is pinning scapularies and medallions of saints to a brassiere for Belén.

LEANDRA: Look at what I'm making for you. I've always had prayers and scapularies pinned to my bra, to remind me of the things I pray for. It always makes me feel protected and blessed. —See, I've pinned a few scapularies for you, so you'll also be protected.

(She shows her the brassiere, which is full of these sacred mementos.)

BELÉN: But my bra looks like a church. Too many saints!
LEANDRA: That's how many you need nowadays.
BELÉN: And these saints are gonna stare at my breasts all day long? Don't you think that's a little sacrilegious?

LEANDRA: They're used to it. They've seen my breasts all their lives. Besides, they're saints and they won't look at them with desire.

BELÉN: Oh, I'm sure this one does. Look at his eyes. What's his name?

LEANDRA: Saint Jude.

BELÉN: The betrayer?

LEANDRA: No. That's another Jude.

BELÉN: Well, he looks like he'll be happy living in my bra.

LEANDRA: Forget it. If there's one thing I can't stand is an atheist, when it only takes a drop of imagination to have faith.

BELÉN: Just a drop?

LEANDRA: And less cynicism.

BELÉN: All right! Show me! But you'll have to take some out.

(Leandra gives her a look.)

LEANDRA: It's all for your protection, hija. This one here . . . this is Saint Christopher, the saint of travelers. If you pray to him, you'll see how Preston Thomas will make it possible for you to leave.

BELÉN: What makes you think he's gonna do anything for me?

LEANDRA: Well, I thought . . .

BELÉN: Well, you thought wrong! . . .

LEANDRA: Why are you so angry my child?

BELÉN: And why are you pushing me into this? Why are you shoving him down my throat? Is it because you felt like a queen the other night, when you sat at his table and he gave you his undivided attention?

LEANDRA: No . . . I . . .

BELÉN: Or was it because he almost applauded your performance and laughed at your obnoxious remarks and paid for your drinks? Do you think he's got something made of gold inside his pants!

LEANDRA: Now you're insulting me!

BELÉN: Insulting you? At least I didn't behave like a hungry hyena that hadn't eaten a meal in three months . . .

LEANDRA: So there was food and I ate! What's wrong with that!

BELÉN: You gorged yourself and you know it!

LEANDRA: You're just angry because the American man . . . !

BELÉN: Because of what? . . . Because he hasn't offered to take me to the states? . . . Because he's not planning to take me with him?

LEANDRA: My child, I feel . . .

BELÉN: I don't care what you feel!

LEANDRA: My child, I can see how you'd be hurt . . .

BELÉN: I don't care for your sympathy!

(Albertina enters.)

ALBERTINA: What are you fighting about?

BELÉN: She's still set on the American taking me up North . . .

LEANDRA: I just said . . .

BELÉN: Yes, it's always the same thing she throws at me. I already know he's leaving and he's not taking me with him.

LEANDRA: So you're bitter because . . .

BELÉN: Do you know what I do when I go see him? Do you know what your niece does?

LEANDRA: No. And I don't want to know.

BELÉN: Well, you should! I use another name that is not my own when I enter his house. That's right, your niece . . . I meet him to fulfill an agreement, to play a fantasy, to play another woman who's not me, except there's no stage where he lives. What we do takes place here, in the mind, in our imagination . . . the same as when you drink a magical potion in a play to dream up another reality. Then we enter his room. And he places me on his bed, in the exact place she used to occupy. And he whispers in my ear what her body used to do—how her heart would move from her chest to meet him there between her legs.

LEANDRA: Stop it, Belén!

BELÉN: No, you hear me out! Then he opens my dress . . .

LEANDRA: That's enough.

BELÉN: He opens my dress and caresses my breasts.

(Leandra sits down, wondering how she could've stopped this.)

Then he enters me and stays there unmoving at first, so I can let him spread inside me, so I get used to him. —You get the picture. I lie to him and I lie to myself. I disguise myself and conceal who I am so I can be part of a world that's different than mine. And it's a dark world . . . but also magnificent, because I can dance and forget the smell of gunpowder that still lingers in the air from the death squads. And all these nights you know what I think to myself, Tía Nanda? That maybe one day something new is going to emerge from all this. That maybe one day he's going to see me for who I am . . . But that's never going to happen, because from the beginning it was always too late . . . always too late . . .

(She walks to Leandra and touches her face gently.)

(Quietly) I don't want you to hate me. I don't want you to be ashamed of me. I don't want to live in shame.

LEANDRA: My child, don't say . . .

(Belén draws back.)

BELÉN: And I don't want you to pity me either. You mustn't feel sorry for me.

(Belén exits.)

LEANDRA: Did you know about this?

(Silence.)

Why didn't you tell me?

ALBERTINA: Because you couldn't have done anything about it and neither could I.

LEANDRA: Well, you're wrong.

ALBERTINA: You were the first to turn a blind eye when the American showed up.

LEANDRA: I just wanted . . .

ALBERTINA: You don't fool me.

LEANDRA: I swear . . . I swear by all the saints . . .

ALBERTINA: Oh, why don't you just admit it! You were just as much of a schemer from the beginning. And there's no point talking about it. *(Beat)* —Don't forget to turn off the lights.

(Albertina exits. Leandra stands motionless, then turns off the light and goes out.)

SCENE 3

Belén and Reforms

Preston's house. Belén enters. She is dressed as Emilia. Preston stands behind her, looking at her through the mirror.

BELÉN: I'd like to be Emilia one last time.

PRESTON: I wasn't expecting this.

BELÉN: Let me be her one last time. —Don't look at me that way. She's always been your point of reference, and without her I would've never met you.

PRESTON: And what good would do this do you?

BELÉN: I'd like to know what she did to forget you and get on with her life.

PRESTON: Are you setting a trap for me?

BELÉN: No. It's not a trap. There was something that you needed to put in order when you wanted me to be Emilia and I helped you. Now do it for me.

PRESTON: It's not the same.

BELÉN: It's your duty. You owe me. Ask me who I am now. —Ask me.

PRESTON: And who are you now?

(She travels to a distant place where she sees nothing but an imaginary night in which she can build her strength. She becomes transfixed by this moment.)

BELÉN: Emilia Naguid.

PRESTON: And where are you?

BELÉN: In the theatre we have created, on the stage where no one else but us watches. Did I come here to see you that last night?

PRESTON: No. I went to see you at the club.

BELÉN: And what color was my dress?

PRESTON: I don't remember.

BELÉN: Black, like this?

PRESTON: Yes, probably black.

BELÉN: And the air? Was it as dark as my dress?

PRESTON: Probably.

BELÉN: Was I alone at the club?

PRESTON: Yes. But when we saw each other, you told me you were with someone else.

BELÉN: Who?

PRESTON: Someone who was never there.

BELÉN: Tell me the exact words you told me.

(She has found her strength and they reenact the moment.)

PRESTON: *And who is that man who leaves you alone in a bar?*

BELÉN: *He's talking to the owner.*

PRESTON: *Good, I'll keep you company until he gets back.*

BELÉN: *No. You shouldn't.*

PRESTON: *Why not?*

BELÉN: *He wouldn't like it.*

PRESTON: *Then we'll tell him I had your legs wrapped around me last night.*

BELÉN: *You're pathetic.*

PRESTON: *And I think you're lovely. How long have you been here?*

BELÉN: *Long enough to want to leave this place.*

PRESTON: *How does he look, this man? Does he allow himself to please you? Does he comply with what you ask him to do? Does he help you like I do?*

BELÉN: *Help me how?*

PRESTON: *The same way I helped you bring back your lover who you couldn't forget.*

BELÉN: *That never happened.*

PRESTON: *Then how come I felt your heart in your hair and your breath when I was deep inside you?*

BELÉN: *No. You only felt someone who became blind and deaf to everything around her.*

PRESTON: *They say the blind only recognize those they're familiar with. Have I changed so much since then?*

(Suddenly she's exposed, disarmed. There is an unexpected tear and she hides it. He knows she is no longer playing her role and she's now in the present.)

BELÉN: Yes, and now I must learn to forget you.

PRESTON: Who are you now?

BELÉN: Belén.

PRESTON: Don't!

BELÉN: Yes. There's a moment you can no longer be the woman who you're trying to imitate, nor can you see yourself wearing a dress that is not your own, nor the silk shoes that don't belong to you.

PRESTON: We had an agreement from the beginning.

BELÉN: I was hoping there was more to it than that.

PRESTON: But I wanted the lie. The game. I was hungry for it. I was dying for it. I wanted it like a drug. An escape. Like a pain you have to revisit to know that you're not dead. Part of it was Emilia. Part of it could've been when I started losing the damn earth from under my feet . . . a sense of place in this country. I couldn't move! I was stuck! I couldn't feel anything. I couldn't even curse my own hell. The truth is I was numb. —Sure, I could've gone back home, just like all the other Americans. They packed their bags the moment they knew that there was nothing left for them here. I could've gone back to Maine or moved to Veracruz and kept the ferries running. But then I saw you . . . and there you were, magnificent, splendid, with your dark hair, emanating a dark hope, spilling out all kinds of desire in me. And I had this mad idea—no—it wasn't an idea . . . it was an instinct that you could help me . . . that you could help me relive what was no longer there. I saw you and something got going again.

BELÉN: The least you could've done is ask me to come with you.

(He grabs her by the arm.)

PRESTON: It's impossible for me to get you out. And even if I could, I couldn't be with you in the States. My life is very different there.

BELÉN: Don't worry. I suspected it.

PRESTON: Look, I never meant to harm you. That was never my intention.

(She moves away from him.)

Belén, come here. Look at me. Let's talk this through. We still have a little time.

BELÉN: And what's a little time? A day . . . an hour . . . A little time so I could pretend to be Emilia again? . . . Or to be less of Emilia and more of myself? A little time so I can learn to reclaim who I was! A little time so I could learn to be without you! To forget all this! A little time to be tempted by snow! What's a little time?!!

(There's a knock at the door. Belén hides her tears. Preston opens the door. Orlando enters.)

ORLANDO: Are Caroline and Oscar here yet?
PRESTON: No. They haven't gotten here yet.

(Silence. There's tension in the air. Preston pours himself a drink.)

ORLANDO: How are you?
BELÉN *(Getting back at Preston)*: Maybe not as good as you.
ORLANDO: Well, I'm very busy.
BELÉN: Yes, it seems as if everything is changing and moving faster than time.
ORLANDO: Yes. It's difficult to keep track of things.
BELÉN *(With irony, trying to hurt Preston)*: Do you find that sometimes people start losing their firmness of judgment? I mean, when everything is changing so rapidly.
ORLANDO: No, the problem is that people are trying to hold on to old ideas and old ways that no longer have any validity.
PRESTON: Well, you know what they say about resignation, that it's a sign of weakness.
ORLANDO *(Grins)*: Sounds like a good phrase for an epitaph, doesn't it?
PRESTON: I don't think I will die any time soon. I still have confidence in the years that lie ahead of me.
ORLANDO: Of course, you're still young and full of ambitions.
PRESTON: We do have that in common, you and I. We are both ambitious, except we differ in our aims and aspirations. You don't hesitate to use force and mediocre means to reach your goals. I tend to be a little more old-fashioned; I have no immediate goals, only determination.
ORLANDO: Yes, it's obvious that you're attached to your Panama hat and your old ways, and I've opted for the beret and military clothes: the future of this country.

(There's a knock at the door. Belén opens the door. Caroline and Oscar enter.)

CAROLINE: Hello, dear.

OSCAR: How are you, Orlando? I'm glad you could come.

ORLANDO: I told Preston I'd be here.

CAROLINE: Well, thanks for coming.

(She gives Orlando a document to read.)

This is the document that was given to us. It was sent to the caretaker.

ORLANDO: Are you aware of the new laws? The Urban Reforms?

CAROLINE: Yes. But they're somewhat confusing.

ORLANDO: Who's the proprietor of the house?

CAROLINE: I am. It was my father's house. He left it to me.

ORLANDO: Does your name appear on the title of the house?

CAROLINE: No, but it appears on the will.

ORLANDO: The house is in the city, right?

CAROLINE: Yes, in the city.

ORLANDO: That complicates matters.

CAROLINE: Why?

ORLANDO: This is not your primary residence, am I correct?

CAROLINE: No, it's always been our winter home.

ORLANDO: And who occupies the house when you're not here.

CAROLINE: The caretaker does.

ORLANDO: You're going to have a difficult time keeping your property or selling it.

CAROLINE: Why? It's my house.

ORLANDO: Not under the new laws of the Urban Reform, and not if your name doesn't appear in the title of the property. And much less if you only use the house a few months out of the year.

OSCAR: That's ridiculous. How can that be?

CAROLINE: Can't we hire an American lawyer that can contest these regulations?

ORLANDO: The present laws in our country have changed the traditional system of inheriting property.

CAROLINE: Wait a minute . . . what do you mean?

ORLANDO: Let me give you an example. Since your father died and you weren't living at his house at the time of his death, the legislation won't give you the right to your father's house.

CAROLINE: That's absurd.

ORLANDO: Look, in plain language it says it here: "Occupants of the unit remain occupants."

CAROLINE: But that's preposterous!

ORLANDO: That's the new law. And you don't live here.

CAROLINE: So the caretaker gets to keep my father's house, because he lives in it all year long.

ORLANDO: That's correct.

CAROLINE: That's insane! We've had this house for over forty years, and my daddy left it to me when he divorced my mother.

ORLANDO: I didn't make the law, señora. But that's what the law requires. The occupant has the right to remain in the house or to sell it, even though he is not related to the deceased owner. —Now, if your house were located on the beach or in the countryside, then you're entitled to your property. You could sell it if you want.

CAROLINE: And why is that?

ORLANDO: Because houses in the city are a necessity as a social service, and we are trying to abolish archaic privileges.

OSCAR: Madonna mía! I don't understand anything! There's got to be a way. This doesn't make any sense!

CAROLINE: Didn't you hear him, Oscar? He just said it. I've lost my father's house.

(Silence.)

ORLANDO: Any other questions?

(Caroline sinks in her chair; her eyes are full of tears.)

CAROLINE: No. We don't have anything else to ask.

PRESTON *(To Orlando)*: I do. Have you accomplished everything you wanted with us? 'Cause you're certainly making a profession of destruction.

ORLANDO: No. We're just taking back what belongs to us, to the people. Good day, Preston.

(Orlando walks to the door and exits. Oscar goes to Caroline to console her.)

CAROLINE: We're archaic. We are old. We are being consigned to oblivion. And we just painted the house, and paid a seamstress to make new curtains. *(There are tears in her eyes)* —You know, this morning when I was washing my face, I heard the dripping sound of the bath taps and I thought to myself, That's the sound I'm going to hear if they take away my house—my father's house crying. *(She hides her tears)* How silly of me, as if a house could cry! Let's go, Oscar. We'll have to find another place for ourselves. Let's start gathering our things. I think the faster we leave, the better it is.

OSCAR: All right. Let's go.

CAROLINE *(To Belén)*: I'd like to see your aunts before we leave. I liked them so much.

BELÉN: I'm sure they'll like to see you, too.

OSCAR: We'll see you later.

(Oscar and Caroline move to exit. Preston walks them to the door then reenters.)

BELÉN: Everybody is leaving.

PRESTON: Do you blame them?

BELÉN: No.

PRESTON: Would you stay in this country if you were in my place?!

BELÉN: No.

PRESTON: Would you stay if everything were taken from you? Answer me.

BELÉN: You know the answer.

PRESTON: Would you stay when you look at the coastline and you see trenches everywhere?! Would you stay if you know that at any moment you could be mistaken for the enemy?! Do you understand my position?

BELÉN: What about those of us who have no other choice?

(He tries to bring her close to him.)

Don't!

(She walks away from him. All of a sudden, what she has been avoiding swells up in her. She begins to weep.)

God! I was hoping this wouldn't happen.

(She tries to hide her tears. She tries to hide everything with a smile, as she gathers her strength.)

It's so much easier being someone else . . .

(She moves to another part of the room and looks into the distance.)

I already know what this place is going to be like without you. I already see the streets without you, the nightclubs without you, the music without you . . . Today when I went swimming, the sea was so blue and crystal clear that I could see all these little fish nibbling my legs, as if they were alerting me and reminding me to look all around me, and take in the beauty of this island . . . and I thought to myself,

If Preston were here, they'd be nibbling and caressing his legs, too. I'm already convincing myself that you're gone. The next day is almost here, and the next, and the next . . . all the days without you.

(She walks out. He stays alone in a pool of light. Lights change.)

SCENE 4

Wearing a Fake Mustache and Farewell

Afternoon. The costume shop. Leandra enters holding a costume. Albertina is offstage disguising herself as man.

LEANDRA: The king popped a button.

ALBERTINA *(From offstage)*: Another one?

LEANDRA: Another one. And I couldn't find it on the stage. You have to help me find it.

ALBERTINA *(From offstage)*: I can't right now. I'm busy.

LEANDRA: If I don't find it I have to change all the buttons.

ALBERTINA *(From offstage)*: I'll help you in a second.

LEANDRA *(Looks at the jacket in the light)*: Oh, who cares if the king is missing a button! He'll just have to do without it tonight. It's almost five and night is already coming our way. *(She gets a hanger and hangs the jacket up on the rack)* God, I'd always start getting the jitters at this time . . . that extra adrenaline we need before we get to perform. Oh well, not good to be reminiscing.

(Albertina enters disguised as a man. She is smoking.)

ALBERTINA: What do you think?

LEANDRA: You look like a fool.

ALBERTINA: I do not. You just don't want me to leave.

LEANDRA: You'll never look like the guy in the photo.

ALBERTINA: Why? What do you mean? I went through hell to get this passport. And it wasn't just getting the passport, it's the visa waiver that's most difficult to get.

LEANDRA: Just take off that silly mustache. Caroline and Oscar are stopping by to say good-bye, and you don't want them to see you like that when they get here.

ALBERTINA: Why not? It will be the ultimate test; if they recognize me, it means the getup doesn't work.

LEANDRA: I can tell you it doesn't work. Just look at your chest. Do you think that wrapping gauze around your two cantaloupes is going to flatten you out?

ALBERTINA: Maybe what I need is a bigger belly.

LEANDRA: You're not going to get through the door of the airport with a dead man's passport and much less through customs. I can't believe that at your age . . .

ALBERTINA: At my age what? At my age I can look more like a man than when I was young. Besides, other people have done it. They've left the country disguised.

(Belén enters.)

BELÉN: ¡Hola!

ALBERTINA *(Imitating a man)*: Hola, Belén.

BELÉN: Hola, Tía Berta.

ALBERTINA: Oh God, she recognized me! I can't believe she recognized me! And I was hoping this would work.

LEANDRA: Why don't you convince your aunt that she looks nothing like the man on that passport she got!

BELÉN: Let me see the passport.

(Leandra shows her the passport. Belén looks at the photo and then at her aunt.)

She's right. You look nothing like this man.

ALBERTINA: All right! All right! Don't terrorize me anymore. I'll go change. I'll go change. And I used to think that the worst thing that could happen to a woman was to look like a man. And now I wish I looked a little more like our father. Lord, and all that time I spent studying all those men in the park, with their pressed shirts and trousers . . . and all for nothing . . . for nothing.

(Albertina takes off the mustache. She is completely devastated.)

How foolish I am! How foolish! I'm stuck in this dungeon! Stuck! Stuck for the rest of my life.

LEANDRA: Come on, change your clothes. Caroline and Oscar are coming to say good-bye.

BELÉN: It's better if I don't see them.

(Belén goes out.)

LEANDRA: It's only Oscar and Caroline.

BELÉN: I'll be in the other room.

LEANDRA: Change your clothes, Berta. *(Albertina doesn't move)* Come on, we'll figure out a way for you to leave. You don't want Caroline to see you dressed like that.

(Caroline and Oscar enter with a bag and a couple of hatboxes.)

OSCAR: We thought we'd drop by before we leave. We wanted to say good-bye.

LEANDRA: How kind of you to come!

ALBERTINA: Pardon my appearance; I was trying on a costume.

CAROLINE: Are you going to be in a play?

ALBERTINA: Ah yes! I am . . .

LEANDRA: Yes. She's going to play the fool in a play. But what a shame Belén isn't here.

OSCAR: Yes, it's a shame we won't be able to see her before we leave.

CAROLINE: Here are a few things I'd like to donate to the theatre. Maybe you can use them in a play. Here are a couple of dresses, and a few scarves and hats.

LEANDRA: Oh, that's very kind of you.

CAROLINE: We wanted to see you again and the airplane doesn't leave till seven.

ALBERTINA: Aren't you going to use the ferry?

OSCAR: Unfortunately, the ferries stay, señora. Preston lost his company and he just left the island.

CAROLINE: And I lost my house. Here's our address in New York. *(She hands them a piece of paper)* Write to us.

LEANDRA: We will.

OSCAR: We'd like to go ahead and be at the airport early.

CAROLINE: Yes, I'd rather leave early and avoid the crowds. There's bound to be lots of people traveling. And I despise farewells, especially seeing all the emigrants heading up North. I'd much rather close my eyes and not have to see the waving hands and the handkerchiefs. Now back to New York. Now back to the cold. No more warm air.

No more palm trees. No more sweet music.

OSCAR: Are you ready, Caroline?

CAROLINE: Ready, my love . . .

(She puts on her glasses.)

OSCAR: The driver is waiting outside.

CAROLINE: Farewell, my dear. We didn't get to know each other that well, but I wish you the best.

LEANDRA: ¡Adiós!

ALBERTINA: ¡Adiós! . . .

OSCAR: Good-bye! Hope we get to see each other again.

ALBERTINA: I'll walk you out. I'll walk you out.

(They exit.)

LEANDRA *(In a loud voice)*: You can come out, Belén. They just left.

BELÉN: No. It's all right. I'll stay here for now.

LEANDRA: Come out, Belén. Look at the things Caroline brought. *(Opens the bag)* A couple of dresses.

(She takes one out.)

They're quite beautiful. Just the style you like.

(She's trying desperately to cheer up Belén. Albertina reenters.)

ALBERTINA: It's nice of them to come and say good-bye.

LEANDRA: Look at these dresses. Beautiful, aren't they!

ALBERTINA: Beautiful. Belén, they're gone.

LEANDRA: And let's look at the hats.

(Opens the boxes and pulls out the hats.)

ALBERTINA *(In a loud voice)*: You should see the hats we got, right out of a store window from Saks Fifth Avenue. We'll be a knockout if we wear them to the Havana Yacht Club.

(Both women put on the hats.)

LEANDRA: She's right. People will think we're American ladies on our way to the Kentucky Derby to see the Run for the Roses. You know they give roses to the ladies attending the Derby party. And the winning horse gets a garland of

554 roses. That's one thing I always wanted to see: a big strong horse with 554 roses around his neck, a symbol of heart and struggle to win the race. That's how we have to be, Belén, courageous and look straight ahead like a horse with blinders.

(Belén enters. Leandra continues to be playful, hoping to cheer Belén.)

How do we look? *(She imitates an American woman)* Miss Smith, what horse are you betting on this afternoon?

ALBERTINA: I'm betting on Lucky Brown. What about you, Miss Wilson? What horse are you betting on?

LEANDRA: I haven't made up my mind. It's either going to be the black horse called Victorious or the gray horse called Orpheus. What about you, Belén? What horse are you betting on?

BELÉN *(Making an effort)*: Probably a nameless horse, one that can run wild.

LEANDRA: Better. Those are always winners.

ALBERTINA: That's the bag with the dresses.

LEANDRA: Will you be home for dinner?

BELÉN: Later. I'm meeting someone.

LEANDRA: Who?

BELÉN: Someone I just met.

LEANDRA: Who's that?

ALBERTINA: Let's go, Nanda. Don't start asking questions.

LEANDRA: All right! We'll go now.

(The aunts exit. Belén takes out one of the dresses and looks at it. A Young Man dressed in military fatigues enters.)

YOUNG MAN *(In a hushed voice)*: Is this a good time?

BELÉN: Yes. Come in.

YOUNG MAN: Is it safe for us to be here?

BELÉN: Yes. I was waiting for you.

(He looks at her through the mirror and touches her shoulder gently.)

YOUNG MAN: Aren't you going to kiss me?

BELÉN: Not until you close your eyes.

YOUNG MAN: What is this, a game?

BELÉN: Yes.

YOUNG MAN *(Playfully closes his eyes)*: What kind of game?

BELÉN: I'd like you to help me see someone.

YOUNG MAN: Who?

BELÉN: Someone who was part of my past.

YOUNG MAN: And who's that?

BELÉN: His name was Preston Thomas.

YOUNG MAN: What kind of a name is Preston?

BELÉN: An American name.

YOUNG MAN: He was American?

BELÉN: Yes. Come close to me.

(He kneels down next to her.)

Let me look at your face. —You have no idea how I've longed to see you. You have no idea how much I wanted to see you. How I've looked for you. How I've looked for you.

END OF PLAY

Hurricane

PRODUCTION HISTORY

A short version of *Hurricane* premiered at the Ringling International Arts Festival at the Asolo Repertory Theatre in Sarasota, Florida, on October 13, 2010. It was directed by Michael Donald Edwards; the scenic and costume design were by Dane Laffrey, the lighting design was by Aaron Muhl, the sound design was by Kevin Kennedy and the special effects were by Pedro Reis; the dramaturg was Lauryn Sasso and the stage manager was Sarah Gleissner. The cast was as follows:

APARICIO	Carlo Alban
RIA	Kim Brokington
FORREST	Paul Whitworth

CHARACTERS

APARICIO: A Caribbean boy, twelve
RIA: A Caribbean woman, late thirties/early forties
FORREST: A European man, late forties/early fifties

TIME AND PLACE

Present time. Somewhere in the Caribbean. A town close to the sea.

We are the memory we retain; without memory, we would not know who we are.

—From *The Notebook* by José Saramago

Scene 1

An Offering to a Forgotten Goddess

Day. The blue color of the sea bathes the stage. We hear the sound of the ocean mixed with an ethereal music. Ria and Aparicio, dressed in white, enter walking slowly. Ria holds a large paper boat full of flowers, an offering to a forgotten goddess who dwells in the profundities of the ocean.

RIA: In the old days, we used to sail out to sea to worship the goddess Yemayá Olokun. Olokun, who lives in the deepest depths of the ocean.

But with the years we stopped worshipping her out in the water, because every time we used to sail to pay our respects and offer our oblations, someone would drown.

(Ria places the paper boat down and watches how it sails slowly on the waters of a blue sea.)

So we became afraid of risking our lives and we stopped our devotion and our worship out at sea. But now we live in fear that one day she will send her waves to drown our islands. And when there is a hurricane we are reminded that she's going to take revenge on us, because we have abandoned her for so long, and she must be so lonely in the middle of the sea, waiting for someone to remember her.

(Aparicio climbs a ladder to look at how the boat floats in the distance. On the other side of the stage, in a different location, Forrest Hunter enters reading the bible and praying that a hurricane doesn't strike this part of the world.)

Accept our gift Yemayá Olokun and keep away this storm.

(She kisses the tips of her fingers and taps the ground three times. She intones an old African prayer. Forrest reads from Jeremiah, Chapter Ten.)

FORREST: Keep away this hurricane, oh God. "Thus we say unto them, the gods that have not made the heavens . . ."

RIA: Yemayá Okuté, Yemayá Mayaleo, Yemayá Ayaba, Yemayá Konle . . .

FORREST: ". . . and the earth, even they shall perish from the earth, and from under these heavens . . ."

RIA: . . . Yemayá Awoyó, the oldest of all the Yemayás . . . the one with the fancy clothes . . . the one who wears seven skirts to battle and defend her children . . .

FORREST: ". . . He hath made the earth by His power, He hath established the world by His wisdoms . . ."

RIA: . . . Yemayá Awoyó, who is far out at sea, guardian of the waters . . . mother with silver hair who gives birth to lakes . . .

FORREST: ". . . and hath stretched out the heavens by His discretions . . ."

RIA: . . . Mother who protects us, unique and perfect woman that protects the seas . . .

FORREST: "... When He uttereth His voice there is a multitude of waters in the heavenss ..."

RIA: ... Caring mother, protect us and save us from death.

FORREST: "... He maketh lightning with rain, and bringeth forth the wind out of His treasures." Amen.

RIA: Amen.

(Lights change.)

SCENE 2

The Winds of the Hurricane

Afternoon. Sound of wind and thunder. A circle of light reveals Aparicio on top of a ladder.

APARICIO: Come, winds, come! Come, winds!

> *(Sound of thunder. Lights reveal Aparicio's parents calling out to him:)*

RIA: Aparicio!
FORREST: Aparicio! Where the hell is that boy?
RIA: I do hope he has enough sense to come home before the winds start blowing too strong.
FORREST: Aparicio!
APARICIO: There they are looking for me, but I won't tell them where I am. —Come, winds! Come to me!
RIA: Aparicio!

APARICIO: They don't know that I'm going to stay here. —Come to me, winds! I'm all yours!

RIA: When he gets home I'll give him a beating he'll never forget.

FORREST: You were the one who told him that men used to fight the winds of the hurricane to gain strength and might.

RIA: And they did. But I didn't think he would take it to heart.

FORREST: So now the boy is out there trying to prove himself.

RIA: This is no time to make me feel guilty. Aparicio! Don't just stand there! Go find him!

FORREST: Aparicio!

RIA: I'll search in this direction and you search on the other side.

(Both Ria and Forrest start looking for their boy.)

APARICIO: From up here I don't hear a thing . . . from up here I see people closing their shops and putting down their shutters. From up here I can see them nailing their doors and their windows shut. They're afraid of the strength of the hurricane. They're afraid of your winds. They pray that nothing happens to them. But I'm not. I'm not. I call out to search for you. You're great and grand! Come and make me into one of the warriors who live in your winds. *(Opens his arms)* Come!

(Ria sees her Aparicio on top of the roof.)

RIA: Aparicio, get down from that roof! Come down right this minute or I'll come get you myself. You come down I said. I promise I won't hit you.

(Aparicio starts to come down from the roof. Once he touches the ground she grabs him by his right ear.)

APARICIO: ¡Ay!

(He pulls away from her.)

RIA: Can't you see that death is out there coming our way! Don't you realize that a storm is heading this way like a raging bull!

APARICIO: I was gonna come home!

RIA: You come home right this minute. You have your father and me looking for you like dogs.

APARICIO: I was gonna come home I told you!

RIA: You ought to be whipped with a belt. Always up in the clouds. Now who knows where your father is. And the hurricane has started to make landfall. Go straight to the house. I'll go look for your father.

(She exits. The sound of thunder.
Lights change.)

SCENE 3

The Day After

Early morning. Spotlight on Aparicio at a makeshift hospital.

APARICIO: Everything started with the hurricane. My mother hid me inside the refrigerator when the winds started to pick up force. She was afraid I might just take off with the storm. My mother hid inside the wardrobe, because she was afraid the strength of the winds would take her away, too. *(Sound of thunder and rain)* The winds were pounding with such force on the front door and the windows, and the rain was coming down so hard on our rooftop that I thought the roof was going to cave in, and the whole house was gonna be destroyed. But my poor father . . . my father was the one who didn't hide anywhere and that's why he is the way he is, because he couldn't find a hiding place.

(The lights reveal Aparicio's father running. He is wearing a dress over a pair of pants. He is confused, lost. Ria runs after him.)

RIA: Forrest, please stop. Let us talk. Forrest, please. Forrest, come back.

APARICIO: That's my father. He is not himself anymore. We don't know what happened to him.

RIA: Forrest, there's no harm in talking.

(Ria can't catch him. She stops in the center of the stage as Forrest runs off. Ria is out of breath and completely disarmed, as she plummets to the floor.)

This is all your fault, Aparicio. If your father hadn't gone out there looking for you this wouldn't have happened to him. See what you've done by being so hardheaded! Nothing can top your damn foolishness this time.

(Aparicio lowers his head.)

And apologies won't get you anywhere. You should be ashamed of yourself. Never a moment's peace with you! And now I have to bear the brunt of this whole nightmare—and all because of you.

APARICIO: Can't the doctors help him!

RIA: Didn't you hear what they said? Your father can't think straight. He has a hard time remembering things. He can't recall certain information they said. The X-rays showed a concussion.

APARICIO: What's that?

RIA: An injury caused by an impact, they said.

APARICIO: How serious is it?

RIA: Serious. Maybe it harmed the function of the brain they said. But they're still figuring it out. That's why he has no recollection of who he was. I just want you to know how grave the situation is.

APARICIO: Will he ever be able to remember things?

RIA: Of course he has to remember who he was. That's what I told the doctor. He was fine before all this happened. Wasn't he?

APARICIO: Yes, he was.

RIA: That's what I told the doctor. He never had any problems remembering things, right?

APARICIO: No.

RIA: That's exactly what I told him. He never did, right?

APARICIO: I don't think so.

RIA: That's what I thought.

APARICIO: At least I don't remember.

RIA: Neither do I.

APARICIO: Unless we're both losing our minds, too.

RIA: No, don't say that. But the mind does play tricks. There are things worth forgetting, and things not worth remembering. They did say he could have a memory disorder. Something called dissociative fugue or amnesia. Or was it cryptomnesia? Crypto-something they said. They told me so many diagnoses, I confuse them all. They also mentioned source amnesia. I think it was source amnesia. Yes. I remember now. Yes, yes, because he can actually recall certain information. But he doesn't know where or how it was obtained. They're still doing memory tests on him. *(Her eyes fill with tears)* Oh, Aparicio, I'm so afraid for him!

(Lights change.)

Scene 4

The Void Etched on His Face

Night. Sound of a cardiac monitor. Spotlight on Forrest: at a makeshift hospital, as he speaks to God.

FORREST: How can I remember the words to express my thoughts when I can't remember who I was or who you were in my life? What's happened to me? How can I forget how to remember? Everything feels foreign to me: my hands, my arms, my legs, my face, my eyes . . . These hands could've been the hands of a pianist or a killer, but I have no recollection of how they served me in life. A man who has no past has no present because he has ceased to exist. I have ceased to exist. *(Looks up to Heaven)* And if I have ceased to exist, have I lost you, too? How can I have lost you?

(Lights change.)

SCENE 5

Her Unreliable Beauty

Morning. Lights reveal Ria powdering her face.

RIA: How do I look, Aparicio?

APARICIO: You look lovely as always.

RIA: You think your father would say that to me?

APARICIO: Yes he will. He'll feel better today.

RIA: In case he doesn't remember me I want to make sure I look beautiful. Imagine if he has to fall in love with me all over again.

APARICIO: He will.

RIA: You say that because you love me, because you see me as your mother. But a person's taste can change overnight, and now, in his condition, he might not like me anymore. Oh no, God forbid. Maybe I should bring him a photo.

APARICIO: What for?

RIA: To remind him of how I looked when he met me.

APARICIO: You probably look the same.

RIA: No, time is ruthless. Can you find me a flower I could wear in my hair?

APARICIO: There are no flowers.

RIA: The hurricane destroyed them, too?

APARICIO: All of them.

RIA: Poor flowers. I used to like wearing them in my hair. Let's go to the notions shop to buy some silk flowers.

APARICIO: The notions shop is all boarded-up and closed.

RIA: That damn hurricane has left us with nothing!

APARICIO: Just wear a ribbon.

RIA: What color?

APARICIO: Any color.

RIA: Some people say that scarlet is the color of love.

APARICIO: Then it would have to be a scarlet ribbon.

(All of a sudden Ria's eyes fill with tears.)

RIA: What if he doesn't like me?

APARICIO: He will, like before. I know he will. Don't worry, Mamá!

(Lights change.)

Scene 6

Swimming Dark Thoughts

Afternoon. Aparicio bathed in a pool of light.

APARICIO: My poor mother. My poor father. It's because of me he is like this. It's because of me this happened to him. I can't stop thinking about it. Last night I could hardly sleep, and when I managed to close my eyes I dreamed of him. He was being swept up in the air by a roaring wind, and he was screaming for his life as he fell into the sea. Then he tried to hold on to a rock, but the sea kept pulling him down to the bottom. And he had to swim for his life, while the big waves were pounding hard against him to drown him. It was so terrible. He couldn't come up to the surface to breathe. —This morning I thought of going to church to confess my sins, but the priest must be busy. The church is full of so many people who've lost their homes that he wouldn't have time to listen to me. And the priest wouldn't do anything except make me repeat ten Ave Marias, which is stupid because then the Virgin would think I'm stuck in one prayer like a broken record. Then I thought of going to the police station and turning myself in for committing this crime, which I really didn't commit, but I feel guilty like a criminal, and I find it hard to live with myself now that my father is like this. And my mother . . . my poor mother, I feel so bad for her, too. My mother who's afraid that my father has forgotten who she is and he won't see her with the same eyes he used to.

(Lights change.)

Scene 7

Forrest Who Is Worthy of His Name and His Past

*Lights reveal Forrest sitting in a wheelchair. Aparicio and Ria enter.
Ria is wearing a scarlet ribbon around her head.*

RIA: Do you recognize me?
FORREST: No. I can't say that I do.
RIA: I didn't think you did.
FORREST: Am I supposed to?
RIA: Yes.
FORREST: Oh.

   (Ria looks at Aparicio.)

RIA: He doesn't recognize us. He doesn't see us.
FORREST: I can see you.
RIA: Yes, but not the way you used to see us.

(She is disappointed and hides her tears.)

FORREST: Why are you crying?

RIA: Because if you had recognized me, you would've welcomed me into your eyes. If you had recognized me you would have kissed me . . . Or maybe you would've said, how are you, my love?

FORREST: Is that what I would've said?

RIA: It's the least I wanted to hear from your lips when I came in. Are you my husband?

FORREST: Am I?

RIA: You don't remember being my husband?

FORREST: No.

RIA: You don't remember ever loving me?

FORREST: No.

RIA: You used to be my husband. My name is Berenice. But people call me Ria, and this is your son Aparicio.

FORREST: Apar-i-cio.

RIA: He is not really your son, because he came to you from the water and you took him in. Are you Forrest Hunter?

FORREST: No.

RIA: What do you call yourself?

FORREST: I thought . . . today I remembered for the first time that my name is Andrea.

RIA: No. That's not the name I met you with.

FORREST: I thought that was my name.

RIA: Andrea is a female name in this part of the world.

FORREST: Am I not a woman?

RIA: No! You're not!

FORREST: I thought I was.

RIA: Why would you say that, Forrest?

FORREST: Today a doctor asked me who I was and that's the answer I gave him. And I thought I did well. Little by little my memory's coming back.

RIA: But that's the wrong memory of who you are. You've never been a woman, at least not in this lifetime. You gave me this ring. It's got our initials inscribed and the date we got married.

(She gives him the ring. He looks at it, then gives it back to her. She pulls out a letter and opens it.)

This is a letter you sent me from India when you went there as a missionary.

FORREST: I was a missionary?

RIA: That's how I met you.

FORREST: I'm sorry. I don't remember.

(He wheels himself to another part of the room.)

RIA: Come back.

FORREST: Come back?

RIA: Yes. Come back. Come back. *(Kneels before him)* Come back to your old self, to who you used to be so you can recognize us, and you can come back to us.

FORREST: Am I mad?

RIA: No!

FORREST: Have I died then?

RIA: No, God forbid! You're very much alive.

FORREST: Then what's happening to me?! What's happening to me?! Was I in an accident?

RIA: Yes, but not a car accident.

FORREST: What kind then?

RIA: There was a hurricane.

APARICIO: You were looking for me—

RIA: We don't really know if you fell down or something hit you on your head.

FORREST: So what do you think has happened to me?

RIA: I just know you're not the same, my love, and you seem to have forgotten who you were.

FORREST: I'm trying the best I can to gather myself.

RIA: I know you are.

FORREST: I try to make a mental map, and sometimes I think it is others who have forgotten who they are. How do you know who you are?

RIA: Well, I . . . I . . . because . . . because . . . I'm still myself. *(Looks at Aparicio)* I'm still the same person I've always been. Right, Aparicio?

APARICIO: Yes, you are.

RIA: And he is still the same Aparicio.

FORREST: Yes, but . . . but how do you recognize yourself?

RIA *(Looks at Aparicio)*: Well, I . . .

APARICIO: We just do.

RIA: Yes, it's not something you have to think about. When I wake up in the morning I recognize myself. And not only do I recognize myself, the morning also recognizes me. And I see and acknowledge who I am in Aparicio, and in God, and in the light that enters through my window, and the objects that sit on our night table. And you can do the same. Can you try to recognize yourself in me, in him?

FORREST: I . . . I don't know if I can.

RIA: Why not? You only have to recognize yourself in our eyes and our hands . . .

(Forrest wheels away from them. Ria and Aparicio look at each other.)

FORREST: Who am I? How was I as a person?

(Ria looks at Aparicio, wanting to find an answer, then glances back at Forrest.)

RIA: Well, you were . . . I've never had to describe you . . .

APARICIO: You were a good father.

RIA: Yes, you were. But it's hard to reduce a person you love to words. And I'm not good with words . . . fancy words, I mean. But you always possessed qualities among the finest a human being can have. Wouldn't you say so, Aparicio?

APARICIO: Yes. The best.

RIA: What else can I tell you, my love? You are my husband and my eyes are blind with love for you. When I met you . . . when I met you . . . you were like light to me. Yes, light, in a world that seemed to be filled with darkness. But you were also shade when light seemed too bright.

FORREST: Can you help me? Can you help me remember?

RIA: I've never taught anyone how to remember, but I . . . I can teach you. If I kiss you, like this, you have to savor the moment, so you can remember it later.

(She kisses him on the cheek. He caresses the place where she has kissed him.)

You see, from now on, you'll remember me in a kiss. And you won't forget me if you recall this kiss.

(Lights change.)

Scene 8

Stains of Memory

Night. Forrest in a pool of light, addressing God.

FORREST: Who is this woman, and who is this boy who are claiming to be my wife and son? How come I don't know who they are? She's kind, this wife I'm supposed to be married to, and so is the boy. But I feel nothing in common with them. I've been asked to write what I know, what I don't know, what I see, what I feel, what I think, what I dream . . . I gather someone will read what I write: a lady in an office who studies memories, a man who studies dreams, handwriting, the memory of words. Maybe no one will pay attention to what I have to say. Or maybe someone will ponder at length my writing, my dreams and deduce some meaning, some logic, since they've also asked me to record my dreams. All I know, this is my third day writing. I guess I'm bound to reveal or say something they want to hear. It could be today, tomorrow or maybe never. *(With frustration)* I just don't know what that is!

(The sound of a train whistle in the distance.)

I only know the days have become formless, shapeless, nebulous ... crowds of people, dirt, dilapidation, destruction, fragments, panic, desperation, dispersion . . . dead trees obstruct the road when I step outside. Why are there so many people with bundles? Why are they praying? Why are they cursing? Last night I had a dream . . . a dream of a young girl crossing the railroad tracks by a train station. And it wasn't just a dream. I recognized the place. I'd been there before. I know that place where the girl was. Who is she?! Who is she?! Who is she?! Who are you???!!!

(The sound of the train whistle fills the space.
   Lights change.)

Scene 9

The Malady of the Father and
Aparicio of Unknown Origins

Lights reveal Forrest and Aparicio in the garden area of the hospital.
Aparicio is holding a basket of food.

APARICIO: I came to bring you food. Mami is coming later. You
　　do remember me, right?
FORREST: Yes.
APARICIO: Do you remember my name?
FORREST: Aparicio.
APARICIO: You gave me that name.
FORREST: I did?

> (*They sit on the ground to eat. Aparicio takes a tablecloth out of*
> *the basket and spreads it on the ground. Then he hands food to*
> *Forrest.*)

APARICIO: Uh-hum. You told me once that the name comes from the word "appear" or "to come into being." You said you gave me this name because when I was a baby I appeared in the mission's backyard when the river flooded. You said you were standing on the roof, after the mission filled up with water, and that's when you saw a baby floating inside a wooden drawer. Apparently the drawer had gotten stuck in one of the branches of the *flamboyán* tree, and that's when you caught sight of me. You told me you dove in the water and saved me from the flood. Mamá says the goddess of the rivers is my real mother. And my real father is the god of hurricanes. —But I don't want to talk about hurricanes.

FORREST: No. Tell me. This is good for me to know.

APARICIO: Well, sometimes I feel . . . it's very strange . . . I feel a pull from the ocean, like a whistling, tempting me to go in the water.

FORREST: How so?

APARICIO: Like a magnet. But I'm afraid if I go in the water something will happen to me and I will never come back. That's why I never try to swim too far out. My mother says the three cowlicks I have on my head is a sign that the god of hurricanes is my real father. You see back here.

(Aparicio turns his head, Forrest touches his hair.)

FORREST: And your mother is superstitious even though she is married to a missionary like me?

APARICIO: Everyone is superstitious on this island. —Would you like olive oil and garlic with your bread?

FORREST: Sure.

APARICIO: It's crazy out there in the streets. It's chaos. So many trees uprooted . . . so much rubble . . . The whole place is a wreck, destroyed, demolished. —Some mayonnaise?

FORREST: No.

APARICIO: People say that nature turned against us with this hurricane and declared war. The winds turned into soldiers and airplanes that fired missiles in every direction, destroying and demolishing everything in sight. Nobody knows where to begin cleaning up the mess. Everyone is shilly-shallying, waiting to see who makes the first move. —You want tomatoes with your sandwich?

FORREST: No.

(They sit on the ground.)

APARICIO: Nothing survived but the damn weeds. And I thought this was gonna save me from mowing the lawn. Everything is out of place in the city. The pharmacy is now the laundromat. The laundromat is now the bakery. Our neighbor's sofa ended up in on our backyard, and their bed at the grocery store. Nobody knows where to begin cleaning up the mess. Our next-door neighbor Isolda, something awful happened to her. She's no longer a seamstress who spends her days sewing buttons and hemming skirts and dresses. Now she wants to swing from the clothesline like a trapeze artist. Her husband had to tie her down to a chair, because she wanted to climb up a street pole and dangle from an electric line. *(Pulls out a salt container)* —A little bit of salt?

FORREST: No. That's fine. How come this happened to this woman?

(Aparicio gives him a sandwich. But Forrest doesn't eat it; he is too lost in his thoughts.)

APARICIO: I don't know. She's obviously fallen off her rocker and lost her mind.

FORREST: You mean like what they said happened to me?

APARICIO: Well, you're not swinging from a clothesline or an electric wire. Thank God you're not. I'd be embarrassed. —Eat.

(Aparicio takes a bite of his bread.)

FORREST: Do you know someone named Andrea?

APARICIO: No. And your name is not Andrea. That's a girl's name.

FORREST: Many find what's happening to me incomprehensible.

APARICIO: I don't. I find it weird. You'll get better.

FORREST: It's at night . . . it's at night that I suffer from a suspicion that there are two beings living within me.

APARICIO: Holy shit! You mean like two people?

FORREST: Yes. And it's at night my suspicion is more present.

APARICIO: How is that possible?

FORREST: Well, I think I am no longer alone in my mind.

APARICIO: You mean there's a ghost and shit like that? —I'm sorry, I know you don't like me to curse.

FORREST: Well, I sort of feel I have a double living inside me. Well, not necessarily a double.

APARICIO: Who then?

FORREST: A young person. Perhaps a young girl.

APARICIO: That's just too spooky, Papá.

FORREST: It's terrible. I look in the mirror and I see my real face and it's different from the one I perceive inside me. Look at me. Do you see the resemblance of a young girl?

APARICIO: No! Of course not! You're my father!

FORREST: But I feel it. My face might not reveal any trace of this being, but I know that my soul is not alone.

APARICIO: It is my fault you are like this.

FORREST: It's not anybody's fault.

APARICIO: If you hadn't gone out looking for me the day of the hurricane this wouldn't have happened to you.

FORREST: Isn't every one of us more than one person?

APARICIO: No!

FORREST: Look, whether I have an angel or a woman inside me, I don't quite know. And you shouldn't worry . . .

APARICIO: But I do! You're my father! Tell me what can I do? How can I help you? What can I do?

FORREST: Promise that you won't let me seem like a fool and be the laughingstock of this town.

(Aparicio embraces him.)

APARICIO: Of course! I promise! I promise! —Pa, I'm sorry. I'm sorry. I'm so sorry. Soon we're going to take you home and take care of you.

(Lights change.)

Scene 10

A Remedy

Morning. Lights reveal Aparicio and Ria. She holds a small bag with a couple of healing stones.

RIA: We have to tell him that if he puts this stone in his mouth, he'll be able to communicate more, and his memory will come back.

APARICIO: And what's this one for?

RIA: If he wears it around his neck it will increase his good judgment and never again will he lose his sense of reason.

APARICIO: What if this doesn't work?

RIA: We try Plan B.

APARICIO: And what is Plan B?

RIA: He needs to experience a fright or something that will make him jump out of his skin.

APARICIO: A fright? How's that going to help him?

RIA: I'm just following orders. If the medicine man said we have to try different things, then we try different things. He did say that when a spirit takes possession of a body these things don't go away overnight, especially spirits who travel in hurricanes. The medicine man said the winds of hurricanes are full of spirits that roam through the air, and they like to take possession of men and women and live in their bodies.

APARICIO: Don't tell me these things, Mamá.

RIA: Oh yeah, it could've happened to you! If you had stayed up there on that roof, you could've ended up like him!

APARICIO: All right! All right! I get it! I get it!

RIA: Don't be stubborn, child! You got to be careful, just like I have to be cautious. The medicine man told me that rainbows carry as many spirits as hurricanes, and women should never leave their houses when there are rainbows, because their spirits fall in love with them and wrap themselves around their hair.

APARICIO: I don't want to hear anymore! You're being superstitious and old-fashioned! Do you want to make me paranoid when I go outside? It's not me who needs a good fright. It's Papá we have to make jump out of his skin. So how are we going to do it?

RIA: I don't know. I'll have to figure it out.

APARICIO: What if he has a heart attack from the shock?

RIA: Why do you always have to think of the worst?

APARICIO: Because it could happen!

RIA: God forbid.

APARICIO: People have died from a shock.

RIA: But that's not going to happen to him. We have to think positive! The thing is to make your father better again! To make him like the man he used to be! And we'll try our best to make that happen!

(Lights change.)

Scene 11

The Lamentable State of Forrest Hunter

Night. In front of the mirror. He combs his hair as he speaks to The Other.

FORREST: No physician has been able to do anything for us. And today we're being released from the hospital. We're being discharged early from our room because the nurses say there are other patients in more critical condition, and the doctor doesn't deem it necessary for a man who is only missing his past to occupy a bed in the hospital . . . and much less to overextend his stay if nothing can be done for him. So, for the time being, my adopted family will take care of us. I say adopted, because I still have no recollection of who they were in my life, and I haven't been able to reconcile myself with my present state, or with you, the other living inside me. You are still a mystery to me. And to accept you is to welcome you blindly . . . and accepting you blindly is the same as accepting death, the voice of madness. What do you want from me? What do you want? What do you want? What do you want?

(Lights change.)

Scene 12

Home Remedies

Lights reveal Aparicio and Forrest.

APARICIO: Let's play a memory game.

FORREST: Like the games I played with the therapists?

APARICIO: More or less the same.

FORREST: What are the rules?

APARICIO: I'll tell you a story and you have to remember some of the details.

FORREST: All right.

APARICIO: Close your eyes.

FORREST: Eyes closed.

APARICIO: So it was eight-thirty at night and Anita, the canary, couldn't sleep, because Oscar, the owl, who likes to foretell the future, told her that today was her lucky day and she should play the lottery.

(Ria enters holding a bucket of water and two towels. Aparicio signals her to come closer as he continues to narrate the story.)

Anita, the canary, had never had any luck, so she didn't want to spend her money on a lottery ticket. But now it was eight-thirty and she was tempted to try her luck, but she had only thirty minutes to buy a winning ticket.

FORREST *(Opens his eyes; Ria stops for a moment)*: What is this, a children's story?

APARICIO: Just pay attention to the details, then I'll ask you questions to see if you remember. Close your eyes.

FORREST: All right. Eyes closed.

APARICIO: So before Anita, the canary, bought her lottery ticket she thought of all the things she would buy if she got the winning numbers. At first she thought she would buy herself a birdhouse with its own private entrance.

(Aparicio signals Ria to move closer.)

Then she thought of buying an apartment in a high-rise building, so she'd be protected from cats and other predators that like to feast on canaries.

FORREST: This canary is ambitious.

APARICIO: Oh you haven't heard anything yet. She also thought of buying one of the Canary Islands.

FORREST: So the moral of the story is?

APARICIO: Well, the canary spent so much time imagining what to buy, that by the time she got to the lottery vendor to buy a ticket it was already too late.

FORREST: And the ticket she would've bought was the winning ticket.

APARICIO: That's right. So the moral of the story: don't count your chickens before they hatch.

(Ria empties the bucket of water on Forrest. He is in complete shock.)

FORREST: What in the world? . . . Why did you do that? . . .

RIA: It's for your own good, Forrest.

FORREST: For my own good? You just emptied a bucket of water on me!

APARICIO: We were told you needed a good fright to shake things up a bit.

FORREST: Well, that's a way to give someone a heart attack.

(Aparicio and Ria start drying him off.)

RIA: We didn't do it to harm you.

APARICIO: Do you feel any different, Papá?

FORREST: Of course, I'm soaking wet.

RIA: No, we mean . . . do you feel any difference?

FORREST: Well, I can remember the canary story.

RIA: But do you feel like your old self again?

FORREST: No. I feel like a wet seal.

RIA: No sign of memory?

FORREST: It's cold. Next time warm up the water.

(Forrest exits. Ria and Aparicio dry the ground.)

APARICIO: He's not getting any better. Yesterday he told me to take him to the sea. He walked by the seashore and talked to himself—no—not to himself . . . I mean . . . he talked to The Other . . . The Other—the one he calls Andrea. Then he danced.

RIA: He danced?

APARICIO: He leapt.

RIA: He leapt?

APARICIO: He splashed the water like a child, a beast. An animal. So, I went in the water and I swam to him. And he told me he was bathing his Other Self . . . the girl. —He's worse than when he was in the hospital. He's gone berserk.

RIA: I don't know what to do. He lives in another time and I don't know what else we can do for him.

(Lights change.)

Scene 13

Tadpoles and a Heavenly Sign

Aparicio stands in front of a clothesline, which is full of hanging white sheets and white shirts. He looks at his reflection in a puddle of water.

APARICIO: All I wanted to do today is run to you, my very own puddle made by the rain, where the tadpoles swim freely. Where it is so peaceful and private, because I can look at my reflection in the water and see the tadpoles swimming happily all over my face. And it makes me feel good and happy, because when they swim in my reflection I start to forget things, like everything that happened to my father. Because the truth is that what happened to him, should've happened to me. I am the son of the hurricane not him. The tadpoles understand all of this. They always understand my thoughts and all of what I am. Last week the doctor did some kind of procedure on me. He drew liquid out of my lungs, because they were filling up with water. A sign . . . a sign that the goddess in the depths of the sea wants me to go to her. Today I think my lungs are filling up again, because I feel short of breath. Sometimes I hang upside down from a tree to see if the water will come out. Or I go for a swim. I figure that if all waters meet, the waves hidden inside my body would want to meet the sea. And, now and then, I have the sensation of breathing under water. A strange sensation that is! Something I can't quite understand. There are days I wonder what color the water inside me is, and if fish could actually live there, and if they could swim in and out of my mouth. Then I could keep them in a glass of water and look at them when I feel lonely and need company.

(Aparicio looks up and addresses the gods of the winds and the goddess of the sea.)

Bring my father back. Bring him back . . . bring him back . . . bring him back to his old self. Hear my prayer, god of hurricanes, god of winds . . . Listen to my prayer, Yemayá Olokun, goddess of the sea. Bring back the man he used to be. His name is Forrest Hunter. He slept on these sheets and used to wear these shirts. Bring him back.

(Ethereal music plays. Suddenly Aparicio sees his father's face projected on the white sheets and shirts.)

If you bring him back I'll give myself to you.

(The image of a school of fish swimming in the depths of the ocean is superimposed on the face of Aparicio's father.)

You can take me with you. Take me with you. I'll give myself to you. But bring him back. Bring him back. Bring him back. Bring him back. Bring him back.

(Aparicio starts to twirl in a ceremonial dance.

We hear the voice of a woman chanting a lament and the sound of the sea.

The images of a dolphin swimming in the depths of the ocean, and Aparicio's father's black suit and shoes floating in the water are now projected on the sheets.

Suddenly, all the items hanging from the clothesline are swept up to the sky by a gust of wind. Aparicio stops twirling and looks at how everything disappears slowly in the blue firmament.

Aparicio is awestruck by the heavenly signs, by the response he has gotten from the gods. He is convinced that his prayers have been answered. Ria, who was standing behind the clothesline, is now revealed, holding a basket of linen. The sight of the flying clothesline mesmerizes her.)

RIA: Where did this wind come from all of a sudden?

APARICIO: I was praying. The gods must have answered my prayers!

(Ria drops to her knees.)

RIA: Blessed be the Divine! *(She looks up to Heaven)* Bring our Forrest back. If you bring him back, I promise to let my hair grow long for a year. Then I'll braid it and cut it and offer it to you, Yemayá, so you can see my devotion. Blessed be your presence. Blessed be God. Blessed be all the saints. Amen.

APARICIO: Amen.

(Lights change.)

Scene 14

Forrest Listens to Bach

Forrest wheels himself in. He has a magazine on his lap and speaks to The Other.

FORREST: The injection has already been administered . . . something called Amobarbital. It gives me a hypnotic feeling, so I'm not turning the world around in my head. Concentration and recollection are still a problem. There's something I'm not doing right. I fail again and again to grasp my past, but that doesn't mean I'll give up on my efforts. I look through photo albums and pictures in magazines to see if I can find a familiar object or a face that can elicit a memory. I do the same with my dreams. The other night you appeared in my dream and I learned you were a cellist. Now when I play my records and I hear Bach or Brahms I imagine that it is you playing the cello.

My family thinks the music is triggering something in me, because they see how the tears roll down my face.

(We hear the music of Bach playing in the background: Cello Suite No. 2, Part One, Prelude.)

So now the music never stops playing at our house. I haven't told them the music makes me think of you, Andrea. They think you're the cause of all my troubles, but they should never suspect that I continue to harbor you in my being. They should never catch me adoring you.

(The magazine falls from his lap as he falls into a deep sleep. Lights change.)

Scene 15

The Color of Memory

Morning. At the beach. The sound of the sea fills the stage. Forrest is relaxing. Ria enters with Aparicio. He holds a beach ball.

RIA: We're going to teach you another way to remember.
FORREST: Does this mean you will give me another fright?
RIA: No. On the contrary. This time we want you to stare at a color, just one color and meditate on it.
FORREST: And what do colors have in common with memory?
RIA: Everything or nothing. It depends on the person and if the color evokes a memory in him. Look at this color. The color is scarlet. The color of love.

(She holds up a scarlet cloth.)

Now let your eyes enter the color.

(Music begins to play.)

And let the secret variations of the color reveal themselves to you. Immerse yourself in the color. Then when you turn your eyes away from the color you'll find different shades of the same color in the most insignificant places. Then you'll have a sense of the substance of memory.

(She lowers the scarlet cloth and puts it away.)

Where do you see the color now?

FORREST: Unbelievable! I see it on your face.

RIA: Where else?

FORREST: I see it on Aparicio's face, too! Underneath the surface of his skin.

RIA: Turn your face and look elsewhere.

FORREST: I see it on that woman's scarf walking by the seashore . . .

RIA: Where else?

FORREST: I see it on that piece of paper by the trash bin.

RIA: Good!

FORREST: I see it on the sign for the ferry.

RIA: Very good!

FORREST: I see it on his beach ball.

RIA: Perfect.

FORREST: And why is it that I see the same color on the waves, if the waves are blue?

RIA: Because color stays within us as a memory. Just let your mind find the color in other places. Let your mind be like a camera that can only photograph this color wherever you see it.

APARICIO: Like this, Papá. Pretend your eyes are a camera.

(In a playful manner, Aparicio pretends to hold an imaginary camera and take a picture of Forrest.)

You just have to hold the camera like this and take a photo. Click. Click. Click.

FORREST: Strange, isn't it? This color has all my attention. Sometimes she's like this. She has all my attention. But for some reason that's not enough. It's not enough for her. *(He realizes he shouldn't have said this)* I mean . . .

RIA: What are you talking about, Forrest?

FORREST: Forget it. I was just . . .

RIA: No, tell us. Tell us.

FORREST: I was just thinking out loud.

RIA: Share with us.

FORREST: She . . . she hasn't gone away . . .

RIA: Who?

FORREST: My companion . . . who is always sending me signals.

(Ria shakes her head, discouraged.)

I'm sorry. I shouldn't . . .

RIA: Is that Andrea?

FORREST: Yes. Sometimes she takes over. She finds me if she wants to. But I cannot always find her.

RIA *(Frustrated)*: Then you should ask her to take care of you like we do.

(She starts to go out.)

FORREST: Ria.

APARICIO: Where are you going, Mamá?

RIA: I don't know.

FORREST: But you'll be back?

(She stops.)

RIA: Not for now.

FORREST: Don't go, Ria.

RIA: I want to go back to the house.

APARICIO: Don't get upset at him, Mamá!

RIA: I can't be all about him, Aparicio!

FORREST: I'm very sorry you are leaving, Ria.

RIA: I'm worn out, Forrest! I get tired of trying! And my mind goes blank, too, just like yours. Others like us want you as much as your Andrea, or whoever the hell she is. But we can't get to you, and it's frustrating and exhausting.

APARICIO: Don't get that way, Mamá!

RIA: Look after him, Aparicio.

FORREST: Don't go, Ria. We will miss you.

(Ria was not expecting to hear this from Forrest. But she refuses to acknowledge what he has just told her.)

RIA *(Shakes her head)*: Oh, Forrest! God knows what goes on in that head of yours. I just don't know anymore.

(She goes out. Forrest doesn't realize why she's leaving.)

FORREST: Why is she leaving? Tell her to come back. Ria, come back.

(Forrest runs after her. Aparicio stays motionless, feeling helpless. Lights change.)

Scene 16

Laughter, Rapture or Delirium

Aparicio squats on the ground. He is holding a jar with a tadpole. We hear the sound of laughter.

APARICIO: Shit . . . Hear my mother laugh. She's laughing again. She does that every morning. She calls it laughter therapy. She thinks it's the only thing that will keep us sane . . . our laughter. I hear her laughing alone inside the bathroom. The laughter rises from her belly like a wave that fills her mouth and her eyes, and then it gushes out of her mouth down to the floor like a cascade. Soon the house will be full of laughter. I bet you anything that she's going to make my father laugh, too. Shit, now there's going to be laughter everywhere, invading everything around us. I told her I don't want to laugh. I don't want to be part of it. I can't . . . I must be serious. If I laugh, I will forget all the harm I've done to my father. If I laugh, the saints will think that everything is fine and dandy in our house and they won't help Papá get better. *(Looks up as if the saints were listening)* I should turn on the mower or the chainsaw, so nobody can hear them laughing and think my parents have gone crazy.

(Ria enters with Forrest. She is being playful.)

RIA: Just do it like me. Come on . . . come . . . *(She tickles him)*
FORREST: Don't . . . don't . . . I'm ticklish . . .
RIA: So laugh . . . laugh like me.
FORREST: I can't. It's silly to do this. It's embarrassing.
RIA: Just try.
FORREST: I can't laugh if I don't have anything to laugh about.
RIA: Come on . . . come on . . . and laugh with me . . .

(She tickles him again.)

FORREST: I can't laugh like that.
RIA: Of course you can. It's good for you. Just laugh with me. Aparicio, come join us.
APARICIO: No thank you.

(Aparicio gets his jar and stays at a distance. Ria begins to laugh again. Her laughter gets louder and louder. The laughter is so infectious that Forrest begins to laugh, too. They both fall to the floor, full of joy. Suddenly, there is silence, and they both sit up and look at each other.)

FORREST: How quiet all of a sudden.
RIA: It's the silence that comes after laughter.
FORREST: I can hear your breathing.
RIA: Me, too.
FORREST: And I can almost hear your heart. Who are you, Ria?
RIA: Who am I? I am you, because, in me, you'll find a little bit of yourself . . . I am you because I can remember how you used to be . . . and, in me, you'll find who you were . . .

(She touches his face) —Forrest, I became your wife before I married you. Life brought us together and married us without ceremony. And, that first night I gave myself to you, was the darkest night of all, because I didn't know how to give myself in the perfection of a bride. But you brought patience with you. —I can be just as patient with you, until you discover yourself and me all over again. —Come to our bed and sleep by my side like before. You don't have to touch me. You can just be by my side.

(She holds his hand and, little by little, she escorts him to the bedroom. Aparicio looks at them full of gladness.)

APARICIO: Now my mother must be happy. If I had money I would go right now to the man who sells cement, and I would buy a truckload full of it, and I would pour it over my mother and my father, so they can always stay together . . . cemented. But who can spare tar or cement to unite two bodies, if there are so many buildings that need repair. *(He lifts his jar)* If only you could blow a bubble big enough to house them and keep them united, undisturbed by the world.

(Lights change.)

Scene 17

Song of Solomon or Calling the Beloved

Night. Lights reveal Forrest. He wears a long, white tunic and begins to recite in a state of rapture and with outstretched arms, part of the Song of Solomon.

FORREST:

By night on my bed I sought him whom my soul loveth:
I sought him, but I found him not.
"I will rise now, and go about the city in the streets,
And in the broad ways I will seek him whom my soul
loveth."
I sought him, but I found him not.
The watchmen that go about the city found me:
To whom I said, "Saw ye him whom my soul loveth?"

(He prostrates himself on the floor and extends his arms out, making a figure of the cross with his body.)

It was but a little that I passed from them,
But I found him whom my soul loveth.
I held him, and would not let him go,
Until I had brought him into my mother's house,
And into the chamber of her that conceived me.

(Aparicio and Ria enter.)

RIA: Forrest, what are you doing up at this hour?
FORREST: Worshipping my beloved.
RIA: But this is not the time . . .
FORREST: It's the only time. At night I am by her side. By day
I'm in the dark.

(Ria tries to help him up from the floor.)

RIA: Come to bed. I don't like to see you like this.
FORREST: Don't take this from me! Don't take it! Don't take it!
Don't take it from me! It's the only thing I have! It's the
only thing I have. It's the only thing.
RIA: I won't. I won't. Come to bed. Come to bed.
FORREST: I know you don't like the way I've changed. I don't
like it either. I would like to fit and be part of the world.
But I've seen that world, past the railroad tracks, and it's a
world that doesn't like me.
RIA: Why are you saying that? . . .
FORREST: Because I've smelled that world, the smell that comes
from homes, the smell of olive oil mixed with onions and
garlic, and it's a world that won't accept me.
RIA: Now you're being foolish.
FORREST: No, you're wrong. I've gone to the place where
I used to work and I don't recognize anybody, and nobody
recognizes me. My face is the same, but they know I'm
not the same person. *(With desperation)* You must listen to
me . . . you must understand . . . the most sacred presence
. . . the most sacred has entered my body, and I feel I have

to be as pure. I know . . . I know I'm not saying what I want to say, or what you would like to hear.

(Almost in a trance) On the night table, there's a man's watch, my watch, it pulses with a beat towards the future, which is no longer my future, because I am no longer the man who owned that watch. And it's difficult for me to cross that line, which contains the past, and turn back in search of that man I used to be. God knows I've tried . . . I've tried . . . but it's too late . . . too late. I have entered a dark sea, Ria, a dark sea and the needle of my compass points to the presence of this girl.

(He becomes desperate, almost ferocious.)

—Don't take away these moments from me! Don't take these moments I have alone with God! Don't take them from me! Don't take them from me! Don't take them! Don't take them! Don't take them! I beg you!

RIA: I won't. I won't. I won't. Hush!

(She embraces him.)

FORREST: I don't like who I've become, Ria.

(Aparicio, full of pain and guilt, leaves the room.)

RIA: I can learn to love you as you are now. I already do. There is something you might not remember about yourself: what you did for us . . . for this town . . . how you built a school and educated children, like Aparicio . . . and what you did for me.

FORREST: And what did I do for you?

RIA: For many years I wasn't able to be private with a man and you accepted this. You were willing to marry me when your family and other missionaries were against it. So how can I not accept you as you are? —I want you to touch me like before when you were my husband.

FORREST: How did we become husband and wife?

RIA: In Milan.

FORREST: What was I doing in Milan?

RIA: It was because of your time in Milan that you surrendered to God.

FORREST: You mean I found God there?

RIA: Yes. And I found you and not God.

FORREST: And how did I meet God?

RIA: It's only recently that I started to remember.

FORREST: Was it difficult for you to remember?

RIA: As difficult as remembering a war, except there was no war in Milan.

FORREST: What do you remember?

RIA: I remember the lies of a German man.

FORREST: What lies?

RIA: He promised me love and to make me into a model in Italy. He told me that Italians were crazy about Caribbean girls that looked like me. He paid for my trip to Italy. In Milan is where my nightmare began. A couple named Günter and Winola picked me up at the airport. They told me that the German couldn't come for me because he had to travel to Munich. They told me I would stay with them until he got back. So when we got to their place, Günter pointed a gun at me and took me to a room. The German man turned out to be a human trafficker and he had sold me like a slave. Two days after that I was sold to another man, an Italian man, who had a brothel on the outskirts of the city. From then on I was forced to give myself to strangers against my will. Then one day you came to my rescue. You told me there was something about me that made me different. You said that I put you in turmoil.

FORREST: In turmoil over what?

RIA: Over everything . . . over everything that went on in that place. You told me there was something about me that changed you.

FORREST: And that's why I got you out of that place.

RIA: Yes. And you saved me from that hell.

FORREST: Was there a girl named Andrea in that place?

(Silence.)

I just want to know if there was a girl named Andrea.

RIA: Yes.

FORREST: So I wasn't able to rescue her.

RIA: No. She couldn't deal with that place anymore. She hanged herself.

(He paces the room.)

I'm sorry. I'm sorry.

(He touches her face. He tries to caress her, but he can't. He feels too dirty and too much guilt.)

RIA: It's all behind us. It's all behind us now.

FORREST: I need to walk. I need to walk.

RIA: Did I do wrong? Did I do wrong in telling you this? Do you understand now why you mean so much to me, Forrest? You saved me from that inferno and I'll always be grateful to you. *(With tears in her eyes)* If it weren't for you, I'd still be paying for my liberty.

FORREST: I need to walk. I need to walk. I need to walk. I need to get out of here. I need to go. I need to go. I'll be back. I need to walk. I need to go. I'll be back. I'll be back . . . *(He exits)*

RIA *(Calling out to him)*: Forrest! Forrest!

(She stays, looking in the direction in which he has just left. Then she goes out to find him.
Lights change.)

Scene 18

A Lighthouse to Project My Father's Face

Aparicio is sitting next to the jar with the tadpole. He has a lighter that he uses to feel the burning sensation of fire on his hand so he can stay awake. He flicks the lighter on, then off, then on, then off...

APARICIO: Damn . . . I know I'm acting like an ass . . . damn . . . fuck . . . fuck . . . it's at night . . . it's at night I have to do this to stay awake . . . Fuck! Who wants to sleep and face the nightmares? *(Picks up the tadpole jar)* You have no worries . . . you don't sleep . . . you don't dream . . . or maybe you do . . . but not me . . . not me . . . I look for excuses . . . I look for ways to stay awake . . . shit . . . Today I was thinking of working at a lighthouse and staying up all night guiding the ships ashore and shit like that, then I can stay up till the wee hours of the morning, and I'd be so tired when I close my eyes that no damn or stupid nightmares will screw up with my dreams . . . Ouch! . . . I could also make use of the reflector in the lighthouse and signal the goddess of the sea to bring back my father's memory . . . and I could also use the lamp from the lighthouse to project slides of his face all across the ocean . . . and maybe I can even project home movies of him . . . of my poor father . . . the father who is not the same . . . then maybe the god of hurricanes and the goddess of the sea will return him to us . . .

RIA (*From offstage*): Aparicio!

(Ria enters.)

Aparicio, didn't you hear me calling?

APARICIO: No.

RIA: Your father is acting strange again. Follow him and keep him out of trouble.

(Forrest enters. He is wearing a long white tunic and is holding a bible.)

APARICIO: I will, Mamá.

(Aparicio starts following Forrest. In real life Aparicio's father would walk for miles on end and his child would follow him. But, here, Forrest walks in circles to illustrate the limitless distance. Aparicio stays in the middle as Forrest circles him.)

Where are you going, Papá . . . ?

(Forrest doesn't hear Aparicio; he is too absorbed in his conversation with God.)

FORREST: Continue walking . . . walk . . . walk . . . as though every step could transcend the slowness of the spirit . . .

APARICIO: Don't walk so fast, Papá . . .

FORREST: . . . Walk, as if with each step we're disintegrating, breaking the darkness all around us . . .

APARICIO: Where are you going, Papá?

FORREST: . . . Walk, as if with each step we're rising above the pull of gravity . . .

APARICIO: . . . Please, don't do any harm to yourself . . .

FORREST: . . . Keep on walking as if we're seeking the lips of the beloved . . .

APARICIO: . . . I don't want you to get hurt . . .

FORREST: . . . Walk, as if our steps were declaring war against any obstacle that stands against us . . .

APARICIO: . . . Papá, listen to me, you have Mamá worried to death . . .

FORREST: . . . on the way to his face . . . his lovely face . . .

APARICIO: . . . I'm not gonna let anything happen to you, you hear me?

FORREST: . . . The sea allowing us to penetrate his eyes . . .

APARICIO: . . . Papá, I'm responsible for you . . .

FORREST: . . . You, my God, my lover . . .

APARICIO: . . . Papá, can't you hear that I'm talking to you? . . .

FORREST: . . . Don't hide from me, my love . . .

APARICIO: . . . Papá, listen to me . . .

FORREST: . . . Where are you, in which house, behind which door? . . .

APARICIO: . . . Don't go so far . . .

FORREST: . . . Where are you, in which wave, in which color? . . .

APARICIO: . . . Let's go back home . . . I'm getting out of breath . . .

FORREST: . . . Your face . . . at last, your face . . .

APARICIO: . . . Let's go back . . .

(We hear the sound of the ocean. Forrest and Aparicio are both getting out of breath.)

. . . Papá, don't go in the water . . .

FORREST: . . . Where are you, in what temple, on what altar? . . .

NILO CRUZ

APARICIO: Please stop!

*(Forrest falls. Aparicio goes to help him get up.
Forrest breaks out of his arms and continues walking.)*

FORREST: . . . Music, it knocks hard at my being . . . enters . . .
APARICIO: . . . You're gonna make yourself sick . . .
FORREST: . . . resounds in my body like an echo . . .

(Forrest falls again. Aparicio tries to help him get up.)

APARICIO: . . . Let me help you . . .
FORREST: . . . Let me be . . . let me find her . . .

(Forrest refuses his help, gets up, and continues his journey.)

APARICIO: . . . You're killing yourself, Father . . .
FORREST: . . . Your words . . . your words, your words resound in
my heart, my skull . . .

*(Aparicio stares at him silently, in a state of shock. We hear the
sound of wind.
    The sound of wind becomes louder. Forrest stops. He's breath-
less. He starts to walk backward, gasping for air. He falls. He
tries to get up and falls again. He tries to get up and falls once
more, in a trance. Aparicio runs to him and tries to help him up,
but his father refuses his help. Then his father gets up and runs
off to the ocean.)*

APARICIO: Don't go in the water, Father! Don't go! Come back!
Come back, Father! Come back!

*(Aparicio doesn't know what to do. All of a sudden, he's inert,
motionless. Then he begins to pray:)*

Don't let him drown! Don't let him drown! Save him,
Yemayá . . . Yemayá Okuté, Yemayá Mayaleo, Yemayá Ayaba,
Yemayá Konle . . .

*(Aparicio sees a giant wave sweep Forrest away. Aparicio runs
off to rescue his father. The sound of the sea becomes louder and
louder as it drowns out everything.*
    Lights change.)

SCENE 19

Aparicio or Apparition

Ria enters. She climbs up Aparicio's ladder. She looks into the distance. She implores Yemayá Olokun.

RIA: Yemayá Okuté, don't let anything happen to them. Yemayá Mayaleo, don't take them with you. Yemayá Ayaba, save them from danger. Yemayá Konle, your waves bring and take the waters, bring them back to me . . . bring them back safe . . . bring them back . . .

(The sound of the ocean and the ethereal music from the start of the play are heard. The whole stage is bathed in blue.)

APARICIO'S VOICE: It wasn't a girl or the face of God that brought my father to the sea, it was Olokun . . . it was Olokun, so I could follow . . . so I could enter the water . . . .the sea . . . so I could visit her in the deepest blue . . . because, in the will of Olokun, there's no such a thing as chance . . . there's only Divine intervention . . . I strived to keep my father from drowning . . . and my father didn't sink . . . he floated like wood . . . and the dark spirit within him was released . . .

(Forrest appears drenched in water. He walks slowly, solemnly, entranced, as if he has seen the face of the Divine. Ria, astonished at seeing Forrest, begins to climb down the ladder.)

RIA: You're back. You're back. You're back. I prayed for you. I prayed so much for you.

(All of a sudden she notices Aparicio's absence.)

Where's Aparicio? Where is he? Where is he?
FORREST: I don't know. I lost him. I lost him out at sea.

(Ria falls to her knees, helpless and disarmed. She lets out a silent cry. Forrest consoles her. We hear faint music and the sound of bubbles rising to the surface from the depths of the sea. We see Aparicio floating, suspended in deep water.
Then we hear Aparicio's voice:)

APARICIO'S VOICE: I've been to the depths of the sea . . . the sea . . . and I visited Yemayá Olokun in her dwelling place . . . and I stared at her . . . she lifted her long hair, which flowed in the water . . . and not only was she a woman . . . she was both male and female, man and woman, goddess and god. She had red eyes, like the eyes of someone who hasn't slept in many years, and the sad gaze of someone who has been alone for too long. *(Suddenly his body is filled with life and starts to swim upward to the surface)* Olokun drew me near, and she pressed against my mouth and swallowed my words, then fed me a wave . . . a restless wave . . . Then I heard her voice cry out: "Awake and be charged with my will . . . with the voice of the sea . . ."

I'm probably the only person who has visited Olokun in many years, and for that she must've been grateful.

(Aparicio, drenched in water, emerges from the sea. He rolls onto the shore in slow motion like an unborn child.)

. . . And like a bubble filled with the breath of the sea, I rose up to the surface and was swept by the current until I reached the shore. For now there won't be any more hurricanes and our islands won't be drowned by the sea. *(He coughs into life and opens his eyes)*
My name is Aparicio and, today, I was reminded that my name means to "appear," "to come into being."

(The orange lights of a sunset bathe Aparicio in a halo. He kneels down full of gratitude, now that life has been granted to him once again.)

END OF PLAY

NILO CRUZ is a Cuban-American playwright whose work has been produced widely throughout the U.S. and Europe. In 2003, he was awarded the Pulitzer Prize and the Steinberg Award for his play *Anna in the Tropics*, and was nominated for a Tony Award. In 2009, he was awarded the Helen Merrill Award and the Laura Pels Mid-Career Playwriting Award, as well as the Fontanals-Cisneros USA Fellowship in Literature.